THE SECRE

THE
SECRET RAPTURE

DAVID HARE

faber and faber
LONDON · BOSTON

First published in 1988
by Faber and Faber Limited
3 Queen Square London WC1N 3AU
Reprinted with corrections 1989

Photoset by Parker Typesetting Service Leicester
Printed in Great Britain by
Cox and Wyman Reading Berkshire

British Library Cataloguing in Publication Data

Hare, David, *1947*–
The secret rapture.
I. Title
822'.914

ISBN 0–571–15408–5

For Blair,
as ever

Only half of us is sane: only part of us loves pleasure and the longer day of happiness, wants to live to our nineties and die in peace, in a house that we built, that shall shelter those who come after us. The other half of us is nearly mad. It prefers the disagreeable to the agreeable, loves pain and its darker night despair, and wants to die in a catastrophe that will set back life to its beginnings and leave nothing of our house save its blackened foundations.

REBECCA WEST

> If you don't like my peaches,
> Why do you shake my tree?
> Get out of my orchard
> And let a poor girl be
>
> POPULAR SONG

CHARACTERS

ISOBEL GLASS

MARION FRENCH

TOM FRENCH

KATHERINE GLASS

IRWIN POSNER

RHONDA MILNE

The Secret Rapture was first performed at the Lyttelton Theatre, South Bank, London, on 4 October 1988.

The cast was as follows:

ISOBEL GLASS	Jill Baker
MARION FRENCH	Penelope Wilton
TOM FRENCH	Paul Shelley
KATHERINE GLASS	Clare Higgins
IRWIN POSNER	Mick Ford
RHONDA MILNE	Arkie Whiteley

Director	Howard Davies
Settings	John Gunter
Costumes	Fotini Dimou
Lighting	Laurence Clayton and Brian Ridley
Music	Ilona Sekacz

ACT ONE

SCENE ONE

Robert's bedroom. The curtain goes up on almost complete darkness. Then a door opens at the back and a dim and indirect light is thrown from the corridor. MARION, *in her late thirties, brisk, dark-haired, wearing a business suit, stands a moment, nervous, awed, in the doorway. She moves into the room which you can just detect is dominated by a large double bed, in which a man is lying, covered with a sheet reaching up over his face.* MARION *stops a moment by the bed, looking down. She then turns to go back towards the door.*

ISOBEL: Marion?
> (MARION *lets out a scream, not having realized that* ISOBEL *was sitting in a chair at the end of the bed.*)

MARION: My God!

ISOBEL: I'm sorry.

MARION: You startled me.

ISOBEL: Don't turn the main light on.
> (MARION *goes to the bed and turns on a small bedside lamp.*)
> I needed some peace.
> (ISOBEL *is younger than* MARION *and blonder. She is in her early thirties, and casually dressed in a shirt and blue jeans. She is sitting at the end of the bed, facing us, not moving. The room is seen now to be panelled, gloomy, dark, old-fashioned. It is absolutely tidy, hairbrushes in place, the body quite still beneath the shroud.*)
> I decided this would be the only place. For some quiet. There's so much screaming downstairs.
> (MARION *moves gingerly towards the bed. She looks a moment.*)

MARION: So were you with him?

ISOBEL: There's actually a moment when you see the spirit depart from the body. I've always been told about it. And it's true. (*She is very quiet and still.*) Like a bird.
> (MARION *looks across, nervous.*)

MARION: Did he . . .?

ISOBEL: What?

I

MARION: No, I wondered . . . who dressed him?

ISOBEL: Dressed him?

MARION: Yes. Is he in a suit?

ISOBEL: I did it. And there was a nurse.

(MARION *stands a moment, not looking at the bed.*)

MARION: Well, I don't know. Are you going to sit there?

ISOBEL: Yes. For a while. Is that all right?

(*She smiles and holds out her hand. But* MARION *does not take it.*)

MARION: Yes. Perfectly.

ISOBEL: Did you want to be alone with him?

MARION: No. I just wanted to see him for the last time.

(ISOBEL *does not move.*)

I'm sorry, you know, I feel wretched not getting here . . .

ISOBEL: Oh, I'm sure Dad didn't mind. He was barely conscious. He had no idea who I was.

(*She smiles.*)

MARION: I was wondering . . .

ISOBEL: What?

MARION: No, it's just . . . no, it's nothing. It's silly. I gave him a little thing. Six months ago. When I . . . when you first told me he was ill. I was shocked. I bought him a present.

ISOBEL: Oh, was that the ring?

MARION: I mean what I'm saying is . . . is he still wearing it?

ISOBEL: No. We took it off.

MARION: Where did you put it?

(*There's a silence.* ISOBEL *finally realizes what* MARION *wants.*)

ISOBEL: It's in the drawer.

(MARION *nods slightly. Then she goes to the chest of drawers and opens the top drawer. She takes out a ring. Then closes it. She moves back across the room.*)

MARION: Well, I must say, Isobel, you've been heroic. I wouldn't have managed it. I know myself too well. The times I came down to see him . . . I'll say this to you . . . it made me uncomfortable. I couldn't be wholly at ease. I find it hard . . . I mean if someone's, you know, as he was . . . I find it hard to strike the right attitude. Don't you find that?

ISOBEL: I don't know.

(*There's a moment's silence.*)

2

MARION: Look, about the ring.

ISOBEL: It's all right.

MARION: Isobel, please let me explain to you . . .

ISOBEL: Honestly, Marion . . .

MARION: I know when I took it just now, it must have looked
bad. Did it look bad?

(ISOBEL *shakes her head.*)

You've always been kind to me. But there are reasons.

ISOBEL: I'm sure.

(*She looks down a moment.*)

MARION: I know what you're thinking.

ISOBEL: I'm not thinking anything.

MARION: Oh, this is awful. It's absolutely ghastly. I knew when I
took it, I should have waited. I should have come and taken
it when I was alone. It's just the thought, if Katherine's got
her hands on it, you know perfectly well she'll sell it
tomorrow – he's left her everything – what, I'm meant to
leave it in that drawer, so she can spend it on drink?

(ISOBEL *looks to the bed, disturbed by* MARION'*s sudden
loudness.*)

For God's sake, I mean, the ring is actually valuable.
Actually no, that sounds horrid. I apologize. I'll tell you the
truth. I thought when I bought it – I just walked into this
very expensive shop and I thought, this is one of the few
really decent things I've done in my life. And it's true. I
spent, as it happens, a great deal of money, rather more . . .
rather *more* than I had at the time. I went over the top. I
wanted something to express my love for my father.
Something adequate.

(MARION *has tears in her eyes.* ISOBEL *is very quiet.*)

ISOBEL: Then by all means you must take it. I can't see why not.

(MARION *thinks about this a moment, looking judiciously at*
ISOBEL.)

MARION: I mean, God, I want to have something. It's a sort of
keepsake. Every time I look at it, I'm going to feel sad.
Because, you know, I think it's going to be a terrible
reminder of . . . what do you call those things?

ISOBEL: A *memento mori*.

3

MARION: But I mean when it comes down to it, it's much better *that* than it's traded for eight crates of vodka for Katherine to pour down her throat.

(ISOBEL *looks at her a moment.*)

ISOBEL: Shall we go down?

MARION: Oh, for God's sake, I can't stand it.

ISOBEL: What?

MARION: Your disapproval.

(ISOBEL *gestures towards the bed.*)

ISOBEL: Marion, please.

(ISOBEL *gestures again, uselessly, unable to express what she feels.*)

I don't disapprove. I'm just upset.

(TOM *appears at the door. He is in his late thirties, in a grey suit of artificial fibre, with a sober tie. He is tall, thin, and his face is boyish.*)

TOM: Oh, you're in here.

ISOBEL: Yes.

TOM: Right.

MARION: Tom, have you unpacked the car?

TOM: I've done that, darling. (*He stands a moment, puzzled.*) Is anyone coming?

MARION: Where?

TOM: Downstairs.

ISOBEL: In a moment.

TOM: It's just a little odd all crowding in here.

(*He frowns slightly.*)

MARION: I'm just furious with Katherine.

TOM: Katherine?

MARION: I mean, have you seen her? She's drunk.

TOM: I'm not sure that's true. I mean surely . . .

MARION: One day, you would think, just *one day*. Was she drunk earlier?

ISOBEL: When?

MARION: You know, when . . . earlier, in his last moments . . .

(MARION *gestures uneasily towards the bed.*)

ISOBEL: I didn't notice.

MARION: I think it's disgraceful.

4

ISOBEL: Well, it hardly matters. Least of all to Dad.

TOM: No, he's fine. He's in the hands of the Lord.

(ISOBEL *frowns slightly at this, then makes as if to leave.*)

ISOBEL: Mmm. Well, perhaps . . .

TOM: Is an ambulance coming?

ISOBEL: No. An undertaker. We have a certificate. That's all been done. Time of death. Cause of death.

MARION: Was Katherine much help?

ISOBEL: What do you mean?

MARION: Was she any help to you? When you were nursing Dad?

ISOBEL: She was fine.

MARION: I bet you had to do everything yourself.

ISOBEL: No. Katherine helped.

(MARION *looks ironically at* TOM.)

MARION: Isobel can't resist being kind about people.

ISOBEL: I'm not being kind. (*She hesitates a moment.*) Also . . . Dad loved her. You must allow him that. He wouldn't have married unless he genuinely loved her.

MARION: You know my views about that.

ISOBEL: Yes, I do.

MARION: An old man was taken for a ride.

ISOBEL: I know you feel that. Honestly, I don't think it matters much. The great thing is to love. If you're loved back then it's a bonus.

(MARION *looks pityingly to* TOM, *as if this were too absurd for comment.*)

He saw himself as a failure . . .

MARION: (*At once*) He wasn't.

ISOBEL: Of course not. But that's how he felt. In the world's eyes. A small-town bookseller. The only thing that distinguished his life – as he felt – was this late passion for a much younger woman. So now he's dead, Marion, you mustn't take that away. (*She turns, a little overcome by her own eloquence. She turns to* TOM.) What do you feel, Tom?

TOM: Feel?

ISOBEL: About what I've been saying?

TOM: I couldn't find fault with it.

MARION: Oh, really?

TOM: I'm sure both of you are right. (*He looks a little nervously at* MARION.) It's wonderful being a woman because you have that knack of knowing what's going on. Men just don't seem to have it. What is it? A sort of instinct? Still, *vive la différence*, eh?

(ISOBEL *is for the first time able to smile to herself*.)

ISOBEL: Yes, well, certainly. Shall I make some supper?

TOM: Oh, I'm defrosting some stuff. I got individual roast-beef dinner-trays from a freezer on the motorway. I didn't think anyone would need more than that.

(ISOBEL *gestures to the door*.)

ISOBEL: So, shall we go?

(*Suddenly* MARION *speaks with unpredicted vehemence*.)

MARION: I'm not going to forgive you.

ISOBEL: What?

MARION: You've tried to humiliate me.

ISOBEL: Marion . . .

MARION: You've made me feel awful. It's not my fault about the ring. Or the way I feel about Katherine. You make me feel as if I'm always in the wrong.

ISOBEL: Not at all.

MARION: Oh, yes. Well, we can't all be perfect. We do try. The rest of us are trying. So will you please stop this endless criticism? Because I honestly think it's driving me mad.

(MARION *turns and rushes out of the room. She is beginning to cry uncontrollably.* TOM *looks down.* ISOBEL *stands, pale.*)

TOM: Well, goodness.

ISOBEL: Oh, dear.

TOM: I'm sorry.

ISOBEL: No. It's not her fault. You lash out in any direction. Marion's in grief. It's her way of grieving. She chooses to lash out at me.

(*She smiles, shaken*.)

TOM: All the time, I must say, we were driving, she was sitting there seething. She kept saying, 'I hope we're not late.' Late? I didn't know what she meant. Then she said, 'I'll never forgive myself if I get there and that ring has gone.' I

6

was rather shocked. But you're saying, what, it's because the death was such a blow?

ISOBEL: I think so.

TOM: And that's her reaction?

ISOBEL: It's a way of coping.

TOM: Gosh, well that's interesting. I do hope you're right. (*He frowns, thinking about it.*) You see, it happens quite often. She gets angry. Why? I mean, she's got everything she wants. Her party's in power. For ever. She's in office. She's an absolute cert for the Cabinet. I just don't see why she's angry all the time.

ISOBEL: Don't you?

TOM: Well, no.

ISOBEL: Do you ever get angry?

TOM: Angry? I don't think so. There's no need to, since I made Jesus my friend.

(ISOBEL *nods slightly.*)

ISOBEL: I suppose that does make things easier.

TOM: Oh, incomparably, yes. He transforms your life if you'll let him.

ISOBEL: Really?

TOM: Oh, yes. And he'll do it for anyone. That's what I like. He'll save anyone. I mean on the surface I was completely unsuitable . . .

ISOBEL: You were never very sinful.

TOM: Oh, God, yes, I was. Oh, yes. Perhaps you didn't notice but I was genuinely disgusting. Still am, of course.

(*He thinks a moment.* ISOBEL *is staring at him.*)

I'm the most horrible sinner. But he forgives me, and that's all that counts. (*He suddenly shakes his head.*) This morning Marion was already on her way to the Department. She's incredible, she's on her way at six, so I get the children's breakfast before I go off to work. Anyway, you called and told me what had happened. I thought, I don't want to break this to Marion on the phone. I'll drive in and tell her in person. I go to the car. Won't start. I open the bonnet. Spark-plug leads have perished. I can't believe it. I think, what on earth am I going to do?

7

Then I think, hey, six days ago an old mate called in and left, in a shopping bag, a whole load of spare parts he'd had to buy for his car. (*He smiles in anticipation of the outcome.*) And, you know, as I go in and look for it, I tell you this, I don't have a doubt. As I move towards the bag. I've never looked inside it and yet I *know*. It's got so I know. I know that inside that bag there is going to be a set of Ford Granada leads. And *then* you have to say, well, there you are, that's it, that's the Lord Jesus. He's there when you need him. I *am* looked after. He wanted Marion to hear the news from me. So that's when he'll decide, right, I'm going to help this person, I'm going to get hold of a few people and just . . . pick them up and move them around.

ISOBEL: What, you mean you think that's why your friend dropped by in the first place?

TOM: Certainly. No question.

ISOBEL: Six days earlier.

TOM: You're right.

ISOBEL: Well, well.

TOM: Of course my friend didn't know. He didn't drop round *knowing*. None of us know when we're part of God's plan.

ISOBEL: Who perished the rubber?

TOM: Oh, that's different. That's a natural thing. (*He smiles.*) People are so full of anger. Really it mystifies me.
(ISOBEL *is looking at him nervously.*)

ISOBEL: Tom, I wonder . . . I wanted a favour. I've no right to ask this.

TOM: Go on.

ISOBEL: It's just, you know how much I love Marion. I wondered if you'd let me know if you sensed . . .
(*She stops.*)

TOM: Please.

ISOBEL: If you felt she was seriously angry with me. If you felt it was serious.

TOM: No problem.

ISOBEL: I don't want you to feel you're betraying her.

TOM: I'll make that promise. I'll let you know.
(*He smiles, full of reassurance.* ISOBEL *looks away.*)

8

ISOBEL: Is the undertaker here?

TOM: I should think so.

(ISOBEL *looks a moment to the bed*.)

ISOBEL: Then we'd better go down.

(*At once we hear* KATHERINE'*s voice. The set parts and we are on the lawn at the back of the house. There is a little garden furniture, seemingly at random. A table with a couple of chairs, then a couple more chairs set further away. Bright sunshine. A warm English day.* KATHERINE *is coming in, in a black suit, with a tight skirt. She is dark-haired, in her early thirties, thickset, pale, quick. Her voice is quite loud.*)

SCENE TWO

The lawn of Robert's house.

KATHERINE: The priest was awful. It was clear he never knew him. (*She sits in one of the chairs.*) To be honest, I was relieved. When the coffin came in, I thought, oh dear, this is going to be unbearably moving. And then mercifully the vicar opened his mouth.

(MARION *appears at the back, now also in black. She walks on and remains standing, thoughtful.*)

It's quite extraordinary. The church must send them on some sort of training course. Called Trampling on People's Feelings.

(TOM *appears, dark-suited.*)

TOM: Do we want a drink?

KATHERINE: Yes, please.

TOM: There's lemon squash. Orange squash. Coffee. Marion?

MARION: Squash. (*She looks significantly at* TOM.) Squash would be nice.

(TOM *turns to go out, as* ISOBEL *appears from another direction, already changed back into blue jeans and a red shirt.*)

ISOBEL: That was my fault.

KATHERINE: It's all right.

9

ISOBEL: I feel terrible. Dad never spoke to a priest in his life. So I tried to give that man some sort of briefing.

KATHERINE: That thing he said . . .

ISOBEL: I know.

KATHERINE: When he said . . . what was the word?

ISOBEL: 'Mr Glass was respected as a local cricket umpire. A task he performed adequately.'

KATHERINE: I mean, really!

ISOBEL: 'Adequately'! It's pretty grudging.

KATHERINE: You might expect better when you've just died.

(MARION *turns, disapproving.*)

Where'd he get that thing about 'known as Ginger'?

ISOBEL: I have no idea.

KATHERINE: He was never known as Ginger. Was he?

ISOBEL: No.

KATHERINE: Not since I've known him.

MARION: He was doing his best. I thought he was very sincere.

(KATHERINE *looks at her a moment.*)

ISOBEL: I stressed forty years of opposition to nuclear armaments. Typical Gloucestershire village. Of course the vicar never used any of that.

MARION: I asked him not to.

ISOBEL: Oh.

MARION: I thought it would be inappropriate.

KATHERINE: It's what he believed.

MARION: Maybe. There's such a thing as a suitable time. Funerals shouldn't have politics dragged into them.

ISOBEL: Is anyone hungry?

KATHERINE: What d'you mean, 'dragged'?

(ISOBEL *is standing, trying to distract them.* KATHERINE *does not turn to look at* MARION *behind her.*)

He didn't want a funeral. The only thing *dragged* in was him. He wanted to be burnt and scattered. He said, 'Shoot me from a cannon into the English Channel.' I'd have done it. It was only at your insistence . . .

(TOM *appears, holding a tray.*)

ISOBEL: Ah good, everyone, look, here's the squash.

(TOM *sets it down.*)

TOM: I don't know what to do. There's a whole lot of people . . .
(*He trails off, gesturing towards the house.*)

ISOBEL: I'll go.
(*At once she goes out to deal with them.*)

MARION: I thought the family made it clear. We wanted some
privacy.

TOM: They've just drifted up.

KATHERINE: Fuck them.

MARION: Katherine, please.

KATHERINE: Fuck them. Let them go somewhere else. Go to
the Drum and Monkey. They can all claim him. It's safe.
Now he's no longer there. (*She turns.*) Well, it's true.
There's nothing people like more than claiming great
friendship with people who aren't in a position to deny it.
It's this immediate appropriation that I find so disgusting.
(*She is suddenly quiet.*) Robert wasn't anyone's.
(*At once* ISOBEL *returns.*)

ISOBEL: They're going to the pub.

KATHERINE: What did I tell you?

ISOBEL: They asked us if we'd like to join them.

MARION: Later. I think we should look after Katherine right
now.
(*Her tone is so threatening that* ISOBEL *shifts uneasily.*)

ISOBEL: Look, Marion, why don't you leave me with Katherine?

MARION: I mean, have you decided?

KATHERINE: About what?

MARION: Tom and I were wondering what you were going to do.

KATHERINE: Oh, that.

MARION: I'm not saying you need to make your mind up
immediately. Perhaps you should go on a holiday first.

KATHERINE: I mean, sure, I'd be happy anywhere, I wouldn't
mind where I went if I could just go somewhere and not
have to put up with *me*.

MARION: Oh, God . . .

ISOBEL: Please, Marion . . .

KATHERINE: Look . . .

MARION: Let me . . .

(There is sudden heat in all this, until KATHERINE *rides in decisively.)*

KATHERINE: All right, look, I know, you all think I'm hopeless. I'm not hopeless. I've had time to think. I do have a plan. I'm not going to stay in this house for the rest of my life. I decided. I'm going to work with Isobel.

MARION: So.

(There's a pause. ISOBEL *doesn't move.)*

Isobel?

ISOBEL: What?

MARION: You didn't mention this.

ISOBEL: Didn't I?

KATHERINE: I want to sell up and, with the money I get, move to London. I think I've got a pretty good business head.

MARION: What does Isobel feel?

*(*ISOBEL *does not turn.)*

KATHERINE: It's just for one reason or another I never had a chance. I left school so suddenly.

MARION: Mmm.

KATHERINE: I wasn't ready. I had this ridiculous relationship with drugs. Which, thank God, I got over. But while that was going on, it was fucking hard to hold down a job. Then I put on four stones. I couldn't concentrate. I was fat and spotty and all over the place. So I never got going. Before I met Robert. And then down here with him, what was there? I helped out in the shop. But that's not really work. I know I'm ready now.

MARION: If Isobel's happy.

ISOBEL: Actually . . .

MARION: What?

*(*ISOBEL *is about to say something, but changes her mind.)*

ISOBEL: No.

MARION: I thought your firm was very small?

ISOBEL: Yes, it is.

MARION: Just the three of you.

ISOBEL: Yes.

MARION: Can you afford another?

*(*ISOBEL *just looks at her, not answering.)*

When did you two decide about this?

KATHERINE: For God's sake, Marion, we haven't decided. There's been a funeral.

MARION: (*To* ISOBEL) Has she even asked you?

(ISOBEL *is silent, reluctant to speak.*)

ISOBEL: Not in so many words.

TOM: Marion, I think . . .

MARION: Well, what do you feel about it?

ISOBEL: Nothing. For the moment. I need time to think. We're all in shock. It's too hard. You think you're ready. Over and over you tell yourself it's coming. But when it happens, it cuts you off at the knees.

(*There's a pause.*)

KATHERINE: Yes, that's right.

ISOBEL: Why don't we talk later?

KATHERINE: God, I need a drink.

TOM: Squash?

MARION: We all need a drink. It's only out of consideration for you that we're not all having one.

TOM: It was Marion's idea. She felt if we all abstained from alcohol, it would be easier for you.

KATHERINE: Well, thank you. (*She pauses a second, savage.*) Any chance of a Scotch? (*Before anyone can respond, she puts her hands up.*) All right, well fine, I didn't ask Isobel. No, I didn't. I assumed. That was wrong. I apologize. However, thank God Isobel is a generous person. I think she knows what I can contribute. She isn't going to say no.

(*At once there is a ringing noise from Marion's handbag.*)

What's that? Is that your handbag?

(MARION *is getting a phone out of her handbag.*)

MARION: Sorry, everyone, I had to turn it back on.

KATHERINE: Can't you leave it off the hook?

MARION: There is no hook. (*She speaks into it.*) Hello, yes, it's all right. The funeral's over. Hold on, I'm going indoors.

(*She walks off towards the house.*)

KATHERINE: I see there's no chance of escaping this Government.

ISOBEL: I heard it all night.

TOM: I know.

KATHERINE: How do you put up with it?

TOM: Oh, I'm not interested in politics.

KATHERINE: No. But you must hear the phone.

TOM: No. Not really. It's just part of Marion. She's just
someone who permanently gives off a ringing tone.
(*He smiles and shrugs.*)

KATHERINE: I just hate it. The idea of what she's doing.
Someone at a party once said to me – they hadn't met
Robert – they said, 'Oh, I hear you've got two step-
daughters.' 'Yes. Marion and Isobel.' They said, 'Where
are they at school?' I said, 'Marion's not at school actually,
she's Junior Minister at the Department of the
Environment.' They looked at me like I was nuts.

ISOBEL: I can see.

KATHERINE: I have to explain to everyone. She's just my step-
daughter. It's absolutely nothing to do with me. What this
Government is. Its loathsome materialism. The awful
sanctification of greed. It's not my fault. That's what I say
to people. I can't help it. Please don't blame me.

ISOBEL: Nobody does.

KATHERINE: Well, good.
(ISOBEL *looks uneasily at* TOM, *who is still standing.*)
It's why I love the idea of joining your business. I like what
you do. Your designs. There's something decent about
them. When I pick up a book with one of your covers – or a
record – I always think, this is something which gives
nourishment to people.

ISOBEL: Some of them do.

KATHERINE: I thought the best thing would be if I came with
you this evening.

ISOBEL: This evening?

KATHERINE: Is that all right?
(ISOBEL *looks quickly to* TOM.)

ISOBEL: What, you mean . . . I hadn't realized . . .

KATHERINE: I don't want to sleep here. The idea . . . now
Robert's gone. I'd like to start work in the morning. Put
this whole thing behind me.

ISOBEL: I'm not sure. Remember, it's all very recent. I think
you should rest – at least for a week or two.
(KATHERINE *looks sharply at her.*)

KATHERINE: What are you saying? You don't want me?

ISOBEL: No, of course not. It's just . . . it's difficult. There's me
and Gordon and Irwin, that's all. The three of us. We're
very small beer. Each of us knows what each of us does.
Inside out. We've been years together. We know each
other's ways. And, to be honest, we're not making a great
deal of money. If we wanted to expand, we'd have to be
sure of the work to pay for it.

KATHERINE: But exactly. That's what I'd do. (*She smiles
enthusiastically.*) I can sell.

ISOBEL: I'm sure.

KATHERINE: That's what I'd be good at. Going to publishers.
Getting you new contracts.

ISOBEL: We know all the publishers. (*She smiles, trying to make
light of it.*) It's a very small world.

KATHERINE: Yes, all right. But I've got a knack.
(*She waits a second,* ISOBEL *lost for an answer.*)
You're saying no.

ISOBEL: I'm not saying no.

KATHERINE: Isobel, for fuck's sake, I need help.

ISOBEL: I know. I know that. I will give you help. So will Tom.

TOM: Absolutely.

ISOBEL: Please come to London, certainly. For a while. You can
sleep on my floor.

TOM: That's a fair offer.

ISOBEL: For the moment I just can't promise you a job.
(*There's a moment's delay, then* KATHERINE *gets up furious.*)

KATHERINE: I'm going to the pub.

ISOBEL: Now, look . . .

KATHERINE: I don't give a fuck. I'm sick of being patronized.
There's only one person who ever believed in me.

ISOBEL: We all believe in you.

KATHERINE: There's just one man who ever gave me a chance.
The rest of you – well, yes, Isobel, in a way you're the
worst. The others don't pretend. But you – it's all this

15

kindness and tolerance and decency. Then just ask for
something, some practical demonstration, just a small act of
faith, then it's no. 'Fuck off.' It's so *fucking* English.
(*She goes out.* ISOBEL *puts her head in her hands.*)

TOM: I'll go after her.

ISOBEL: It's all right. They won't let her in. She's been banned
for life from the Drum and Monkey.

TOM: (*Puzzled*) Isn't she English herself?
(ISOBEL *is suddenly exasperated.*)

ISOBEL: Oh, God, it makes you feel so powerless. I saw all this
coming. I saw it weeks ago. And I just delayed doing
anything. I thought, just leave it, I've got more than
enough. Nursing Robert. I was doing almost nothing.
Most of the time I was just holding his hand. Often as he
slept. Once in a while, Katherine would put her head in.
She'd kiss him on the forehead. I remember thinking, as
she bent over the bed: when Robert dies, the trouble will
start.
(MARION *comes back in.*)

MARION: What's going on?
(ISOBEL *ignores her, not noticing her.*)

ISOBEL: And there's *nothing* you can do. You can see it coming,
and you still can't do anything.

MARION: Katherine's going mad.

TOM: She won't get into the pub.

MARION: She's in the kitchen. She seems to be taking up
floorboards.

ISOBEL: Oh, God, she must have a hiding place.
(MARION *anticipates* ISOBEL*'s departure by shaking her head.*)

MARION: It's too late. She's already got it.

ISOBEL: I thought I'd looked everywhere.

MARION: She says you won't give her a job.

ISOBEL: Well, I can't.

TOM: I'll go.
(TOM *goes out towards the kitchen.* MARION *is looking at*
ISOBEL *with disdain.*)

MARION: How can you have been so incredibly stupid?

ISOBEL: What was I meant to do?

MARION: I'd have thought it's fairly obvious. You have to pretend.

ISOBEL: Pretend? Pretend what? That I have lots of money? That I don't have any partners? That we don't all have to work alongside each other, three to a rather small room?

MARION: Why didn't you say, 'Well, I don't know yet. Come to London.'

ISOBEL: That's exactly what I said.

MARION: Keep her calm. String her along.

ISOBEL: I tried.

MARION: *Lie* to her.

(*There's a moment's pause.*)

ISOBEL: No.

MARION: Why not?

ISOBEL: Because I can't. She pushed me. I could have said, 'Yes, fine, there's a job.' But there isn't. She'd have found out pretty quickly. What's the point of lying? (*She looks at* MARION *a second.*) Anyway it's wrong.

MARION: Well, that's it.

ISOBEL: What?

MARION: There you are. *That's* what it's about. That's why she's crying in the kitchen. With a bottle of whisky in her hand. Because *you* can't understand there are actually more important things in life than your wretched sense of honesty.

(ISOBEL *looks at her, not rising to the charge.*)

ISOBEL: Well, in that case why won't *you* offer her a job?

MARION: Don't be ridiculous. I'm in the Conservative Party. We can't just take on anyone at all.

ISOBEL: What, and I can?

MARION: It's different.

ISOBEL: How?

MARION: You know perfectly well. It's quite a different world. With extremely high standards of intellect and conduct. Civil servants have an extremely competitive and highly ordered career structure. In which you get very few marks for being an abusive alcoholic.

ISOBEL: Oh, so you think she's just right for me.

(MARION *shakes her head, angry.*)

MARION: No, it's you who always says there's nothing wrong
with her. You always say, 'Oh, she's fine. Just restless.' But
when the moment comes . . . that's the end of your so-
called principles. You're so like Dad.

ISOBEL: It's nothing to do with principles. (*She sits down, lost.*)
I'd just like to be sure we do the right thing.

(KATHERINE *returns, silently. She appears quite quickly, then
moves towards them, a new gentleness in her manner.*)

KATHERINE: Well, this is much nicer. I apologize. I was being
shitty. (*She leans over the top of* ISOBEL's *chair and kisses
her.*) Isobel.

ISOBEL: It's fine.

(*Characteristically, she takes* KATHERINE's *hand for a few
seconds.*)

KATHERINE: I've spoken to Mrs Hurley. I was in the kitchen.
Lunch will be ready in three-quarters of an hour. She's
planning a rabbit and vegetable pie.

(*Suddenly* TOM *appears. He has obviously been running in
pursuit of* KATHERINE. KATHERINE *smiles.*)

I outsmarted him. I've hidden the bottle again.

TOM: I'm sorry, Marion. I tried.

(MARION *looks at him unforgivingly. Now* KATHERINE *is
suddenly emotional, the alcohol flowing round in her and coming
out as tears.*)

KATHERINE: It gives me confidence, and I must say today I
should be allowed a little confidence. Given what lies ahead.
(*She smiles bravely, wiping her eyes with her sleeve. She sits
down.*) I met your father first in the Vale of Evesham. Yeah,
he stopped one night in a motel. It was appalling. I don't
know how I'd ended up there. I was working the bar.
Trying to pick men up – not even for money, but because I
was so unhappy with myself. I wanted something to
happen. I don't know how I thought these men might help
me, they were travellers, small goods, that sort of thing, all
with slack bellies and smelling of late-night curries. I can
still smell them. I don't know why, I'd been doing it for
weeks. Then Robert came in. He said, 'I'll drive you to

Gloucestershire. It will give you some peace.' He brought me here, to this house. He put fresh sheets in the spare room. Everything I did, before or since, he forgave. (*She sits, tears in her eyes, quiet now.*) People say I took advantage of his decency. But what are good people for? They're here to help the trashy people like me.

(MARION *looks disapprovingly from the back.*)

MARION: Well, I suppose that's one way of looking at it.

(*There's a pause.*)

ISOBEL: Katherine, I'll take you tonight.

KATHERINE: No, really.

ISOBEL: You say you want a job. You can start with me tomorrow.

KATHERINE: That's very nice of you, Isobel.

(ISOBEL *looks at her warily.*)

ISOBEL: I'd like to feel it would mean you gave up the whisky.

KATHERINE: I can't promise. I can promise I'll try.

(ISOBEL *stands. She smiles.* KATHERINE *gets up and embraces her.*)

Oh, Isobel.

(TOM *stands admiring the couple in each other's arms.*)

TOM: Perfect.

MARION: I must say I'm pleased.

(MARION *and* KATHERINE *embrace now.*)

Katherine.

TOM: Praise the Lord.

MARION: What?

TOM: No. Nothing. I'll shut up.

(*The three women look at him. He stands a moment, cheerful, embarrassed.*)

I'm sorry. It just slipped out.

(*At once the sound of* IRWIN's *voice, almost overlapping as the scene is replaced by Isobel's studio, which is a room half office, half studio, in which there are three dominating draughtsmen's desks, each with its own stool. Late evening. The lights are burning.* IRWIN *is returning to his desk with a sheet of tracing paper.* IRWIN *is an apparently modest man, in his late twenties, his curly hair smartly cut short. He wears blue jeans, more or less*

19

identical to ISOBEL's *and a coloured sportshirt. He is calling offstage to someone we do not yet see.*)

SCENE THREE

Isobel's office.

IRWIN: I've got everything on file. I can't help it. I file everything. I even filed at school. (*He sits at his desk and resumes working.*) Every scrap of paper. Everything in place. I don't know what it means. Someone once told me it meant I was prematurely middle-aged.
(*Now we see* ISOBEL *joining him, carrying two cups of coffee, one of which she sets down by his desk. She is still in her jeans, but with another sportshirt which is only subtly different from* IRWIN's.)
ISOBEL: Well, I don't like to say. I mean, about the filing.
IRWIN: I know.
ISOBEL: And do you keep private things?
IRWIN: Certainly.
ISOBEL: I'll bear that in mind.
(*She smiles and goes to her own desk, where she also begins to work.*)
IRWIN: It's silly. I even have a file marked 'Smashed Dreams'.
(ISOBEL *smiles.*)
ISOBEL: Give me an example.
IRWIN: There was a waitress . . .
ISOBEL: I haven't heard this.
IRWIN: I was seventeen.
ISOBEL: What was she like?
IRWIN: She was great. I painted her, actually.
ISOBEL: I've never seen that.
IRWIN: Yeah. She has veal parmigiana in one hand and kidneys turbigo in the other. With peas. I was very keen on colour in those days. And she had one of those actual

20

uniforms – like twinkies, you know? The black and white
costume. With the colour of the food. The composition was
excellent.

ISOBEL: And what was the dream?

(IRWIN *smiles*.)

IRWIN: The dream was – oh, you know – we'd have a cottage
in Suffolk. We used to go to Liverpool Street, and buy
all the local papers. Search through. Even now when I
hear the words 'East Anglia', it's like a hand enclosing
my heart.

ISOBEL: What happened to her?

IRWIN: She left me. And I put six months of copies of the *East
Anglian Daily Times* on a file.

(ISOBEL *looks across at him a moment, thoughtfully*.)

IRWIN: I call it the sad file. When something goes wrong, I clear
the papers up and put them in the sad file.

(ISOBEL *has got down from her stool and is now standing behind
him, looking at his work*.)

ISOBEL: It's very good.

IRWIN: I like the gun. I'm pleased with it.

ISOBEL: I like the wound.

IRWIN: Oh, really? (*He hands her a photo*.) I used Reagan's. I
found it in a paper. I looked at Kennedy's. But it was too
much.

(ISOBEL *is looking thoughtfully at the photo*.)

ISOBEL: The only thing I remember is, Alexander Haig ran
through the White House, screaming, 'I'm in charge! I'm in
charge!'

IRWIN: It was funny.

ISOBEL: I know. But I have to tell you – this is shocking – it's the
only time I've ever found a politician sexy.

IRWIN: God!

ISOBEL: I know.

IRWIN: That is really not good.

ISOBEL: I know. It's appalling. It makes no sense to me. It annoys
me. (*She smiles*.) There ought to be some justice.

IRWIN: (*Quietly*) That's right.

ISOBEL: There is no justice. A woman responds to the most

deplorable things.

(She stands a moment. They are both completely quiet, not looking at each other. Then she blushes bright red, looking down.)

IRWIN: You're blushing.

ISOBEL: No, I'm sorry.

(She looks away, half giggling, very embarrassed.)

I was thinking of something you do.

(There is a contented silence. Neither of them move or look at each other.)

IRWIN: *(Quietly)* Do you think we'll have a child?

ISOBEL: Mmm. There's a fair chance of it.

IRWIN: Will you marry me?

(ISOBEL turns and looks at him.)

Will you marry me now? If I ask?

ISOBEL: I think we *will* get married.

IRWIN: Uh-huh.

(He sits, thinking.)

ISOBEL: It's something Dad said – for no reason – a few days before he died. Absolutely no reason. It was weeks since I'd mentioned you. He only met you once. He said, 'Will you marry Irwin?' I said, 'Yes, I rather think I will.' *(She suddenly looks up, sharply.)* What's that? I heard something drop. *(She goes to the door and opens it, picking up an envelope as she does.)* It's a note.

IRWIN: Is anyone there?

ISOBEL: No. They've gone.

(She closes the door, having looked down the corridor. She opens the envelope and reads. IRWIN hunches down over his work.)

How extraordinary. It's from Gordon.

IRWIN: Oh, yes?

ISOBEL: He says if he sees me, I'll dissuade him. But he's decided it's time to move on.

(She looks up.)

What's going on? Did he talk to you?

IRWIN: Just a little.

ISOBEL: Did he tell you he was going?

22

IRWIN: Not in so many words.

ISOBEL: He seemed so happy. What does he feel?

(IRWIN *looks uneasy, hesitates.*)

Is it Katherine?

(IRWIN *doesn't answer. But* ISOBEL *is surprisingly calm and gentle when she speaks.*)

Why didn't you tell me if that's what it is?

IRWIN: Because, really, it's none of my business. He was slightly put out, it is true.

ISOBEL: I should have asked him first?

IRWIN: Not that. You know she's quite difficult.

ISOBEL: She's impulsive.

IRWIN: Yes. Also she's proprietorial. We work very hard, the money isn't brilliant . . .

ISOBEL: I'm trying to improve it.

IRWIN: I know. I'm not criticizing. But before Katherine came, Gordon had job satisfaction to compensate. And I think he probably felt that had gone.

(ISOBEL *thinks a moment.*)

ISOBEL: (*Decisively*) I'll call him up.

IRWIN: Also – let's be fair – it was always a bit odd, even before Katherine came. He was in love with you.

ISOBEL: You think so?

IRWIN: I haven't any doubt.

(ISOBEL *looks at* IRWIN *uneasily.*)

ISOBEL: He never said.

IRWIN: Of course not. He was fifty. And looked like Sydney Greenstreet. He was also very sweet. My guess is he'd never loved a woman. He was absolutely charming to me. He never let on, or behaved as if he was jealous. But that sort of thing takes a toll.

ISOBEL: I don't understand it. (*She stands, trapped and angry. Then suddenly lets her anger out.*) Oh, shit, I knew. Of course I knew. But what can you do? It's really impossible. Is it the same for all women? People get a fix. You do nothing, absolutely nothing. You're just chatting, you're just walking round the room. And then suddenly, for no reason, they're looking at you as if you're away to the races! (*She stands a*

moment, shaking her head.) Gordon, I mean! It's ridiculous!
We've nothing in common.
IRWIN: Well, no. He's smart, he knows that. So think about it.
That makes it worse. He's living at a certain level of pain.
But there are privileges. Like, he sees you every day. You
give him your attention. Things are pleasant. And stable.
Till Katherine.

(ISOBEL *is suddenly quiet, looking at* IRWIN.)

ISOBEL: You seem to understand this. Do you feel the same way?

(IRWIN *puts down his pen, serious.*)

IRWIN: It's different for me.

ISOBEL: Why?

IRWIN: Because we're together. I have you.

ISOBEL: So you mean you'll put up with Katherine?

IRWIN: Partly. (*He looks down.*) Anyway, now it's a practical
question. Who'll do the books?

ISOBEL: Well, she can. Can't she?

IRWIN: Accounts? Katherine?

ISOBEL: Katherine can do maths. She's not incompetent.

IRWIN: It's just we used to be running a business. Now you want
us to do social work.

(ISOBEL *stands, brought up short by what* IRWIN *has said. She
looks at the telephone.*)

ISOBEL: I can't call him. Not if that's the situation. Oh fuck, why
is everything so *hard*?

(*She stands, lost.* IRWIN *watches her a moment.*)

IRWIN: What actually happened at the funeral?

ISOBEL: Oh . . .

(*She waves a hand uselessly.*)

IRWIN: I didn't like to ask before.

ISOBEL: No. I didn't like to say.

IRWIN: You never said anything. You just came back with
Katherine.

ISOBEL: I haven't had time to decide what I feel.

IRWIN: How was Marion?

ISOBEL: All right. (*She laughs in anticipation of her story.*) Did I tell
you, they're building a swimming pool in their back garden?

IRWIN: That sounds very nice.

ISOBEL: That's what I said. Till I realized it's for Tom to do his conversions. I was looking at his suit trousers, I noticed they were wrinkled. He said they're always like this. It's because he wades in. If you look carefully round his chest, you can see a sort of watermark. I said, why can't you baptize people in swimming trunks? He said, the Lord expects a certain level of decency.

(IRWIN *is smiling*.)

IRWIN: What did Marion think about Katherine?

ISOBEL: Oh. She was desperate I give her a job.

(IRWIN *looks at* ISOBEL *significantly*.)

Don't look at me like that.

IRWIN: I'm sorry.

ISOBEL: I hate it. What are you thinking?

IRWIN: I don't know, I wasn't there at the funeral, I can't gauge. But it seems to me everyone landed her on you.

ISOBEL: No, it's not true.

IRWIN: Does Marion like her?

ISOBEL: Of course not.

IRWIN: Well!

ISOBEL: That's not the point. I just feel – she hasn't said this – I just know that if I tried to get rid of her now, it would be disastrous for her self-confidence. She's just lost her husband. She couldn't face the future. She was frightened. She was lonely. If I hurt her now, it'll put her right back on the drink.

(IRWIN *pauses, doubtful*.)

IRWIN: Yes, I'm sure, but . . .

ISOBEL: What?

IRWIN: Isn't that a form of blackmail? I've had friends who've been through all this. The threat is 'put up with everything I do, or else I'll drink again'. Don't alcoholics just drain everyone around them?

ISOBEL: Yes, but she's stopped. She *ex*-alcoholic. She's been here three weeks and not touched a drop.

IRWIN: Not in front of us.

ISOBEL: That's really unfair.

(*There's a pause*. IRWIN *looks down*.)

We're doing something for her. We're helping her. She's
happy here. I know all the problems. But we can't just pull out
of it now.

(IRWIN *smiles*.)

IRWIN: Do you want to go to bed?

ISOBEL: No. I did. I wanted to, ten minutes ago.

(*They are both smiling*.)

What are you laughing at?

IRWIN: Now Katherine's climbing into our bed.

(*At once* KATHERINE *comes in. She is wearing a large coat, and
underneath it a smart shiny blue dress. Her arms are full of
flowers*.)

KATHERINE: Flowers! Flowers! Flowers for everyone!

(*She dumps armfuls down on the table, then takes some across to*
ISOBEL.)

Look, Pacific orchids. They're incredibly rare.

(*She sets these down beside* ISOBEL, *then starts to take off her coat*.)

ISOBEL: What on earth's going on?

KATHERINE: The man's outside. I've bought his whole stall.

ISOBEL: What time is it?

IRWIN: Nine.

KATHERINE: Do you have any money? The wretched man's
followed me. I've said I'll go back tomorrow.

ISOBEL: Irwin?

(IRWIN *shrugs slightly and goes out to pay the man*.)

KATHERINE: I walk that way every day. Why can't people *trust*
you? Stupid little man.

ISOBEL: What are you celebrating?

KATHERINE: I've sold the house.

ISOBEL: Dad's house?

(ISOBEL *stands astonished as* KATHERINE *now searches for vases
in the cupboard*. IRWIN *returns, wallet in hand*.)

IRWIN: It was seventy pounds. It's cleaned me out. Do you want to
write me a cheque?

KATHERINE: Don't worry. I'll do it tomorrow.

ISOBEL: When did you sell it?

KATHERINE: Today. To a sucker in computers. Just think, I'll
never have to go back.

(IRWIN *frowns and goes back to his work.*)
I'm going to get a flat in London with the money. I saw a place just round the corner from here. Only nicer. I just passed it with Max.

ISOBEL: Max?

KATHERINE: You know, the publisher.

ISOBEL: Of course I know Max.

KATHERINE: The man I went to see. And – listen – he says he will consider giving us exclusivity. We can do all his covers for an eighteen-month trial period. An exclusive contract.

IRWIN: Really?

(IRWIN *looks at her doubtfully.*)

KATHERINE: Well, ring him. That's what he said. Mind you, it was fucking hard work. I had to take him to dinner. I was crossing and uncrossing my legs. I thought I'd have to make the ultimate sacrifice on behalf of the company. (*She has moved across with a jar of flowers to where* IRWIN *is working.*) What's this? The *Encyclopaedia of Murder*?

IRWIN: Yes.

KATHERINE: No, that isn't right. There should be an exit wound. And that's not the effect.
(*She puts the flowers down.*) Look, give me a pencil. There's one here.
(IRWIN *grabs his drawing from the board before she can write on it.*)

IRWIN: Leave that.

KATHERINE: Why?

IRWIN: Just leave it.

KATHERINE: I'll show you. Look, another piece of paper. A bullet goes through like *this*. Do you see?
(IRWIN *goes to the other side of the room, very deliberately.* ISOBEL *is still standing in disbelief.*)

ISOBEL: You sold the house?

KATHERINE: Yes.
(IRWIN *now holds up a book, his voice raised.*)

IRWIN: I actually bought a book. I went to the library this morning, I may say before you were awake, you were snoring on the floor . . .

KATHERINE: Point taken.

IRWIN: It's called *Criminal Pathology*. (*He points to it.*)

ISOBEL: Irwin, hold on.

IRWIN: It has a series of extremely lurid photographs. Which I have copied with photographic accuracy.

KATHERINE: Yes, can I say something I've been longing to say? I think that may be the trouble with your work. Its very accuracy. I've got a very different idea of art. I think the artist should *add* something. He should add an extra layer. That's what you're not quite doing in some of your stuff. (*She shakes her head slightly.* IRWIN *is watching her, saying nothing.*)

You're very bound, you're very *earthbound* by all this accuracy business.

(ISOBEL *attempts to intervene.*)

ISOBEL: Please, both of you, can we hold off on this?

IRWIN: Now look, hold on, just a moment, you said this picture wasn't accurate?

KATHERINE: That's right.

IRWIN: Then you said I was too restricted by accuracy.

KATHERINE: That's right also. It's incredible. You're losing both ways. (*She smiles at the irony of it.*) The funny thing is, Max was saying at dinner . . .

IRWIN: Were you two talking about my work?

KATHERINE: . . . he wanted to give us a contract because he was so convinced I could bring something out in you. Maybe something you didn't even know was there.

IRWIN: Well, I'm sure *that's* true.

(ISOBEL *speaks with sudden emphasis.*)

ISOBEL: She's sold the house.

IRWIN: What?

ISOBEL: Our father's house. She didn't ask us.

(*There is a pause.* KATHERINE *seems offended for a moment. Then goes to get more flowers.*)

KATHERINE: (*Casually*) What's wrong? I rang Marion. She said the whole deal was fine.

(IRWIN *looks across at* ISOBEL, *his earlier point proved.*)

I wanted to check I was asking enough money. So I knew

Marion was the right person to ask.

IRWIN: Did Marion call you?

(ISOBEL *shakes her head, her voice now very small.*)

ISOBEL: Marion hates the house.

KATHERINE: Certainly she said she was never going to use it. I said I could never face going back. (*She smiles sweetly at* ISOBEL.) That only left you. (*She stops now, serious.*) I have no money, Isobel. It's as simple as that. Robert and I spent everything he earned. He had no investments, he didn't approve of them. He thought they were wrong. So do I. It's immoral, all that disgusting trading in shares. He just bought books. I loved that in him. His other-worldliness. The way he just didn't give a damn about money. But now of course we've got to pay for that other-worldliness. The bill's come in. We've got to pay duties. (*She looks sadly down.*) And I knew you wouldn't want me to starve.

ISOBEL: No.

(ISOBEL *looks at her.* KATHERINE *looks back, the two of them staring at one another. Then* KATHERINE *suddenly cheers up.*)

KATHERINE: I'll make some cocoa. Then I'll come back and tell you everything that happened at dinner.

(*She goes out.* IRWIN *waits, tactfully, for* ISOBEL *to speak.*)

IRWIN: Isobel.

ISOBEL: I know. Don't say anything. (*She shakes her head.*) What are they doing? I wish someone would tell me what's going on. (*She looks a moment to where* KATHERINE *has gone.*) For a start it's only three weeks ago. Are we not allowed to *mourn*? Just . . . a decent period of mourning? Can't we have that? Can't we sit quietly? Why on earth is everyone running around? (*She looks to* IRWIN.) I watch my family now, it's like they have to be *doing*, it doesn't matter what. Run around, sell this, change that. The day he died, I was sitting in his room, just trying for a moment of stillness. In came Marion. (*She shakes her head.*) Can't we have a moment of grief?

(IRWIN *looks at her, as he has for the past moments, and now, tactfully, moves over to her.*)

IRWIN: Isobel, they're cutting loose. Now you've got to.

ISOBEL: What do you mean?

IRWIN: They're saying the whole thing is over. Your father's dead. There is no family. You're the only person who's still hung up on it. Don't you see? (*He kneels beside her, his tone gentle.*) You have to let go.

ISOBEL: But what does that mean?

(IRWIN *looks her in the eye.*)

IRWIN: Sack Katherine.

ISOBEL: Irwin, I can't.

IRWIN: You must. It's a farce, what she's doing. What she just said about Max.

ISOBEL: I know. Don't.

(*She shudders in horror.*)

IRWIN: The idea that Max . . .

ISOBEL: Oh, don't.

IRWIN: This lovely old man would sit at dinner while Katherine made a play for him. It's appalling. Katherine leaning over the table in that awful dress. Her bosom hanging out. I mean it's actually funny. It'll make us a laughing-stock. And for what? (*He pauses a moment.*) Because you have some misplaced sense of duty to your father.

(ISOBEL *turns and looks down at him.*)

Isobel, you owe her nothing. Get rid of her now.

(ISOBEL *looks at him a moment, then shakes her head.*)

ISOBEL: There was something there for Robert. I can't just abandon her. Think, there was this middle-aged man. Very idealistic. Living a life of ideas. 'Yes, I know,' he said, 'Katherine's impossible. But without her I'd have had a much less interesting life.' (*She smiles.*) He said that living with Katherine was like being on manoeuvres with a great army. You had no idea where you'd wake up the next day. Once he woke up at four. She was in the kitchen with a drinking friend. She had a gun in her hand, and was yelling, 'Go on, do it! Do it! I want you to! Go on, if you love me shoot me in the leg!' He loved that story. He didn't mind what people called her awfulness. She was prepared to say what she thought, especially to all those people he didn't dare be rude to himself. That's what he loved. She wasn't

30

dependent on anyone's opinion. (*She smiles.*) You know what it was? He thought she was free.

(IRWIN *is bewildered, assertive.*)

IRWIN: But she *isn't.*

ISOBEL: Of course not.

IRWIN: She's chronically dependent. Mostly on other people's good will. What you're describing is what more usually is called bad behaviour. And it's always at somebody else's expense.

(ISOBEL *looks at him a moment.*)

ISOBEL: Mmm.

IRWIN: All you're saying is, she found a sucker.

ISOBEL: It made him happy.

IRWIN: That's not the point. It won't make you happy. Will it?

(ISOBEL *pauses again.*)

ISOBEL: No.

IRWIN: Then that's it. You have no choice.

(*She looks at him. Then reaches and puts her hand on his cheek.*)

ISOBEL: I don't want to do it. Not tonight. I want to bury my head in the sand.

IRWIN: You can't do that.

ISOBEL: Why not?

(*She smiles. He kisses the back of her hand. At once she kisses him. He puts his arms round her, the feeling warm between them.*)

I like it. I've got great plumage.

IRWIN: I've seen your plumage.

(*He smiles.* KATHERINE *calls from the other room.*)

KATHERINE: (*Off*) Isobel! Isobel!

IRWIN: But you must do something now.

(KATHERINE *returns with a huge vase of flowers beautifully arranged. She is already talking.* IRWIN *gets up and tactfully takes them from her.*)

KATHERINE: Did I tell you . . .

IRWIN: I'll take those from you.

KATHERINE: Tom said he wants to make an investment in the firm?

ISOBEL: In us?

KATHERINE: Yes.

ISOBEL: How extraordinary! He's never said that before.

KATHERINE: No. Well, he feels now I'm here, the whole thing's a much better bet.

(ISOBEL *frowns*.)

ISOBEL: But why? I can't see we need it.

KATHERINE: If we're expanding, I mean like if Max comes through, you're going to need extra artists. We're going to have to pay them.

ISOBEL: Where would we put them?

(KATHERINE *waves hand, confidently*.)

KATHERINE: Oh, we'd get a bigger place. In the centre of town. If we expand now, get some capital investment, we could be making money like hay. (*She laughs*.) Everyone else is.

ISOBEL: I'm not sure.

KATHERINE: I admit, it all depends on me. I've got to keep Max's cock hot in my pocket. But you shouldn't worry. Tonight I made a pretty good start.

(ISOBEL *looks quickly to* IRWIN, *who is standing watching*.)

ISOBEL: Look, I'm sorry, Katherine . . .

(*She stops, unable to go on*.)

KATHERINE: What?

ISOBEL: Max is my friend. I'm also very close to his wife. Who's called Julia. Max gave us our very first job. It's just incredibly offensive when you talk of him as if he were a prostitute's trick. (*She pauses again*.) You make me sound priggish. But it's a difference of style.

(KATHERINE *looks at her. She nods a little, suddenly quietened, sincere*.)

KATHERINE: This isn't going to work. I felt it. I really did my best.

ISOBEL: I know.

KATHERINE: I put such effort into this.

ISOBEL: I know you did, Katherine. I'm not attacking you. I'm just saying we go about things different ways.

(KATHERINE *smiles at a memory*.)

KATHERINE: Yes, it's something Robert said. He said, 'You must always remember Isobel is very *narrow*. She has no vision.' That's right.

(IRWIN *stirs uneasily.*)

IRWIN: I'm sure he didn't say that.

KATHERINE: It's all right. I won't tell you any more of what he really thought. I promise you, I'm going to leave quietly. My shouting days are over. It's up to you to say. I'm not totally insensitive. Do you want me to leave?

(ISOBEL *looks in agony to* IRWIN *for help.*)

ISOBEL: Look, it's just I have lost Gordon . . .

KATHERINE: We're not talking about Gordon. I'm asking *you.*

(ISOBEL *stands unable to answer. Then suddenly* IRWIN *intervenes.*)

IRWIN: The answer is yes.

ISOBEL: No.

IRWIN: Isobel just doesn't want to say it.

ISOBEL: Irwin, please.

(*He holds up a hand. Stops. Looks steadily at* KATHERINE.)

IRWIN: We've just been talking. She's just too nice to say. I'll say it for her. She's been taken advantage of. She's desperate you should go.

(*There's a pause.*)

IRWIN: Look . . .

KATHERINE: That's fine. Well, that's very clear. Thank you, Irwin. If you let me sleep here, I'll go in the morning. I'll say goodbye then.

(*She turns and goes out, silently.* ISOBEL *does not move.* IRWIN *waits.*)

IRWIN: Well, there we are. Can we go to bed now? Isobel?

(ISOBEL *turns and looks at him blankly.*)

Come on.

ISOBEL: Don't be ridiculous. No.

(IRWIN *turns and goes to the desk, silently. He picks up the drawing and screws it into a ball. He throws it down into the wastepaper basket.*)

What's that?

IRWIN: No, she's right about the drawing. I'll start again. My work is tenth-rate. (*There is a pause.*) Isobel. Please. Let's go to bed.

(ISOBEL *turns and looks at him.*)

ISOBEL: I can't do this. She's got to stay.

(ISOBEL *goes out after her.* IRWIN *turns towards us, his face darkening.*

Then the sound of women's laughter as the scene is replaced by MARION *coming on in a pearl-grey suit, followed by* RHONDA, *a dark girl in her early twenties, with a great shock of long black hair, extremely lively and attractive, but with rather an academic disdain. They come from the garden into the living room of Robert's house, which is in the process of being stripped out. There is a bare wooden floor, no curtains, an odd selection of abandoned chairs, which are mixed up with the open packing cases which are scattered round the room. But the library is still complete: walls of books from floor to ceiling. At the back a high, long line of windows gives out on to the lawn. It's early afternoon. The women are in great spirits.*)

SCENE FOUR

Robert's living room.

MARION: Well, I must say I really enjoyed that. I can't remember when I had such a good time. I am actually good at it. I do actually enjoy a good political session.

RHONDA: Oh yes, absolutely. I thought you were absolutely superb.

MARION: Did you think so?

(MARION *stands, reliving the encounter.* RHONDA *flops down in a chair.*)

I don't like Greens. They're so self-righteous.

(KATHERINE *comes into the room from the hall. She is wearing a sweater and black trousers. She is carrying a book.*)

Hello, Katherine.

KATHERINE: How are you?

(*She sits down to read her book in this half-empty room.*

34

MARION *goes on as if she has been asked a question.*)

MARION: I had to see a delegation. Those awful Greens. Green people. About radiation levels from nuclear power stations. A subject, I may say, about which I know a great deal more than they do.

RHONDA: That was clear.

MARION: They're always going on as if their case is moral. That's what annoys me. Ours is moral too. People need power. Nuclear power is a cheap and effective way to provide it. It gives a lot of ordinary, decent people a considerably improved standard of living.

(ISOBEL *appears in the doorway.*)

I think that's pretty *moral* as well.

(*She turns and sees* ISOBEL, *frowning. She has in her hands piles of old books for the packing cases across the room.*)

Isobel.

ISOBEL: Who were those people?

MARION: Greens. I said I'd meet them. I wanted to impress on them I had a country background. So I had the idea of showing them this house.

(*She smiles.* RHONDA *smiles too.*)

ISOBEL: Where do they come from?

MARION: London.

RHONDA: Yes. It was brilliant. We said, 'You *can* meet the Minister. Of course. The Minister's happy to meet you. But wouldn't it be more appropriate to meet in the countryside?'

ISOBEL: I see.

RHONDA: It meant they had to drive down.

MARION: I was going to be here anyway.

(*She shrugs. The two of them are grinning.*)

RHONDA: You know her parting shot?

ISOBEL: I don't.

MARION: It's just I hate exaggeration. That and self-righteousness. Those two things. I said, 'Come back and see me when you're glowing in the dark.'

RHONDA: Brilliant.

MARION: I'd invited a journalist. His pencil went crazy. It's so easy. It's like throwing fish to seals. I was giving him the headline for his story. 'Minister Says Come Back When You Glow.'

(RHONDA *laughs again*.)

ISOBEL: Isn't that a little bit risky?

MARION: What?

ISOBEL: I mean, I don't know, isn't it a little bit extreme?

MARION: It's a *little* bit extreme. That's why it's brilliant. That's the whole art of publicity for a politician. You roll back the boundary just that little bit. A year ago you couldn't have said it. But now – let's face it – everyone hates Greens. (*She sits down contentedly*.) They're bored. It's a seventies problem.

RHONDA: That's right.

(MARION *points at* RHONDA *from across the room*.)

MARION: I despise their briefing. I'm so much better briefed. You know, they had absolutely no understanding of the method of accounting for plutonium rods. I cottoned to that. Something that man with the blue shoes said very early on . It was a very small slip. But I got it. (*She smiles at* RHONDA.) From that moment on, they were dead.

RHONDA: Very good.

MARION: You know, they were expecting an idiot. That's the first mistake. Because you're a Conservative. And a member of the Government. They expect you to be stupid.

RHONDA: That gives you an advantage.

MARION: Yes, that's right. (*She turns and cuts the air decisively with her hand*.) You blast them right out of the water. Hey, at this moment I could take them all on. The gloves are off. That's what's great. That's what's exciting. It's a new age. Fight to the death.

(IRWIN *has come in. He is wearing gumboots which in a moment he will sit down to take off. The sound of distant gunfire*.)

IRWIN: God, the countryside. You do forget, don't you?

ISOBEL: What?

IRWIN: Hello, my love. (*He kisses her cheek before going to sit down*.) Saturday afternoon. It's like the trenches out there. Bang! Bang! Bang! What is it about country people? They want to kill everything that moves.

(KATHERINE *looks up for the first time*.)

KATHERINE: Irwin's back. Are we ready for the meeting?

MARION: Let's get Tom.

(*She nods at* RHONDA *who at once leaves the room on her errand*.)

IRWIN: We don't do it in London. We don't say, 'Great, let's go out and shoot some cats. That would be *fun*. Murder some dogs for exercise.'

(RHONDA *sweeps back into the room*.)

RHONDA: He's coming.

IRWIN: Outside the cities England seems to be one big rifle range.

(*At once another explosion of gunfire and* TOM *comes in, carrying a black briefcase, which he is opening on the way*.)

TOM: Right, everyone, I have the proposal in here.

(ISOBEL *smiles, trying to make a joke of how brisk everyone has suddenly become*.)

ISOBEL: Oh, Lord.

TOM: Are we ready?

RHONDA: Should I go?

MARION: No, of course not.

(TOM *has already walked over to* ISOBEL *and handed her papers*.)

TOM: This is the form. You would sign this.

ISOBEL: Thank you.

TOM: And this. Incorporation. Transfer of title.

(MARION *has walked across from the other side and is already offering a Mont Blanc*.)

MARION: Pen?

ISOBEL: Thank you.

(ISOBEL *looks round. The whole room is suddenly waiting for her:* KATHERINE *in her chair, book on knee,* RHONDA *leaning against the bare wall,* IRWIN *looking at his gumboots,* TOM *and* MARION *standing on opposite sides of the room*.)

TOM: Please go ahead. Ask anything you like.

(ISOBEL *smiles, embarrassed, trying to keep the atmosphere light. In the distance the guns fire again*.)

ISOBEL: Well, I mean, you know I've already hinted, I don't mean to be difficult, it's just Irwin and I . . . (*She turns to him*.) Do you want to speak first?

(IRWIN *shakes his head*.)

We both feel . . . I don't know how to say it . . . what you're
suggesting is a very big step.

TOM: It's a big step for us.

ISOBEL: Of course.

TOM: My company has the spare money. We want to use it. We
want to help your firm expand. Because, well, our motives
are wonderful. We happen to believe in you.

ISOBEL: Yes, well, that's jolly good. It's just . . . the *form* of the
arrangement.

MARION: Isobel's worried about the idea of a board.

(TOM *frowns*.)

TOM: Oh, I see.

MARION: She's used to owning her own firm.

TOM: Yes, but surely you'd expect us to protect our investment?
(*He stands a moment, genuinely puzzled*.) I don't think there's
anything sinister in that. It's pretty normal practice.

ISOBEL: Your company would own us?

TOM: Well, yes, indirectly. They wouldn't interfere. After all
you'd have a board of your own.

ISOBEL: Of which you'd be chairman?

TOM: Technically.

ISOBEL: And of which I would simply be one single member?
(TOM *frowns again*.)

TOM: You'd also be managing director.

MARION: (*Firmly*) Isobel, Tom is President of Christians in
Business. I think that makes it pretty clear he's a man you
can trust.

(ISOBEL *turns at once, upset*.)

ISOBEL: Oh, God, yes, please, honestly, this mustn't be
personal . . .

TOM: (*Shyly*) It isn't.

MARION: He's Chairman of his church's Ethical Committee.

TOM: We meet six times a year. We try to do business the way
Jesus would have done it.

ISOBEL: You mean, had he come to earth in a polyester suit and
with two propelling pencils in his top pocket?

TOM: I'm sorry?

(MARION *looks angrily across the room*.)

MARION: Isobel's making a joke.

TOM: Oh, I see.

MARION: Tom is out there in the community. He runs all these schemes. For youth. Don't you, dear?

ISOBEL: Of course. Tom's honesty is not at issue. (*She stops a moment, having trouble now. She tries to speak quietly.*) It's just I fear I'd be losing control.

(*There's a short silence. The guns fire again.* KATHERINE *looks up, speaks quietly.*)

KATHERINE: Isobel, you *are* the business. Everyone knows that. You are its asset. With all respect to Irwin. You are what makes it work. No one is going to replace you. (*She shrugs.*) The whole board thing is just a technicality.

(ISOBEL *shakes her head, frustrated now, beginning to get angry.*)

ISOBEL: Why don't you just *give* me the money?

MARION: I find that question unforgivably naive.

(*Suddenly* MARION *has flared up, a sister reminded of old arguments.*)

ISOBEL: Now look . . .

MARION: No, I . . .

ISOBEL: (*Exasperated*) Perhaps I don't *want* to get bigger.

MARION: Don't be ridiculous. Are you crazy? There's money to be made. Everyone's making it.

TOM: Remember, God gives us certain gifts.

MARION: Tom is right.

TOM: And he expects us to use them. That's our duty. If we fail to use them, he gets angry. Justifiably. God says to himself, 'Now look, why did I give that person those gifts in the first place? If they're not willing to get out there and make a bit of an effort?'

ISOBEL: I *am* using them.

TOM: Yes. But not to the full.

(ISOBEL *looks at him a moment, across a hopeless gulf.*)

MARION: It's just the time. You must feel it. It's out there. It's the only thing I regret about belonging to the Government. Unfortunately I've got to help drive the gravy train. I'd rather be clambering on the back and joining in the fun.

ISOBEL: What fun?

MARION: Making money.

KATHERINE: Darling, everybody is.

MARION: Please wake up.

(KATHERINE *is suddenly animated*.)

KATHERINE: You know I think this Government's appalling. But on the other hand, let's face it, given what's going on, it's just stupid not to go and grab some dough for yourself.

MARION: It's more than stupid. It's irresponsible.

KATHERINE: I mean, give it to the good guys. That's my philosophy. If we don't make the money someone else will. Well, in my book the arseholes have had it their own way long enough.

(ISOBEL *smiles*.)

ISOBEL: But isn't there a chance that taking some will turn *us* into arseholes?

(RHONDA *laughs*. KATHERINE *smiles at her, compassionately*.)

KATHERINE: Oh, Isobel . . .

ISOBEL: Well?

KATHERINE: I think I can live with that danger. Can't you?

(MARION *is moving quietly to the far side of the room*.)

MARION: If you don't take the money, then you insult us.

ISOBEL: Now, Marion, come on . . .

MARION: It's like saying you don't trust us.

ISOBEL: You know that's unfair. You mustn't say that.

MARION: I don't know how else to interpret a refusal. You're saying you don't think your brother-in-law will look after your best interests. (MARION *turns away, letting the accusation hang damagingly in the air*.) I don't know. Perhaps that's what you feel.

ISOBEL: No.

(ISOBEL *looks to* IRWIN, *desperate for help, but his eyes are still on his feet. The guns fire in the distance. Then* MARION *is very quiet*.)

MARION: Also, you know, you must think of other people.

ISOBEL: I'm sorry? (*She looks at her, not comprehending*.) What?

MARION: I sometimes think, what sort of life is it if we only think about ourselves?

(ISOBEL *looks round the room.*)

ISOBEL: I'm sorry, Marion, you've lost me.

MARION: Katherine.

(She is looking across the room to where KATHERINE *now has modestly folded her hands in her lap.* ISOBEL *is quite still.*)

ISOBEL: Ah, yes.

MARION: That's who I mean. I don't know, it's difficult . . . Katherine, do you mind if I say?

KATHERINE: Go ahead.

MARION: One of the reasons Tom is so eager to put money in, is to help Katherine through this very difficult time.

ISOBEL: I see.

MARION: To me, let's face it, what's the best thing to happen to this family? In many, many years? The way Katherine's coped with bereavement so magnificently.

*(ISOBEL *stands, her lips tight together.*)*

I don't think you'd deny her a seat on the board.

(There is a silence. ISOBEL *goes slow, sensing a trap.*)

ISOBEL: No. Well, of course not . . .

MARION: Would you?

ISOBEL: Don't be silly.

*(KATHERINE *is quite still.*)*

If the scheme goes ahead, of course, it's agreed, Katherine would be part of it.

MARION: Good. *(She smiles to herself.)* Tom and I love the idea of Katherine having a long-term directorship. It's just the kind of security she's lacked in her life. *(She shrugs slightly.)* I mean, again, it's your decision. Katherine won't mind. Will you, Katherine?

*(KATHERINE *shakes her head.* ISOBEL *turns now to* IRWIN.*)*

ISOBEL: That leaves only one person. Irwin?

IRWIN: Yes?

ISOBEL: What you were saying last night.

*(IRWIN *looks up mildly from his boots.*)*

Irwin thinks it's folly to mix family and business.

IRWIN: I do think that. Normally, yes.

ISOBEL: What d'you mean, 'normally'?

IRWIN: I don't know, I can see, I've been listening, it's all very tricky . . . (*He finally puts his boots decisively to one side.*) Let's face it, Isobel, we are a bit stuck. We do need capital . . .

ISOBEL: Irwin . . .

IRWIN: Tom is cash-rich. From making paper napkins. Or whatever he does.

(TOM *smiles tolerantly.*)

It seems you would be getting a great boost. As far as I can see, with very few strings. The best way – I was explaining this to Tom and Marion this morning – to get good work in our field is to leave people alone and allow them some breathing space. (*He smiles confidently.*) Tom agrees with this. So it's not in his own interest to interfere in any way.

(MARION *looks across the room, pleased.*)

MARION: Also Irwin did mention, you don't mind my saying this . . .?

IRWIN: What?

MARION: He did think perhaps you were hoping to get married.

ISOBEL: *Married?*

IRWIN: No!

ISOBEL: Did Irwin say that?

MARION: Irwin, you've landed me in it. Was that a confidence?

IRWIN: Isobel . . .

MARION: Now you're being coy.

IRWIN: I said no such thing. Honestly.

ISOBEL: Irwin, what have you been doing?

MARION: I can't really see what's so wrong with the idea.

ISOBEL: Please, Marion . . .

(MARION *holds up a hand in surrender.*)

MARION: All right, disregard marriage, forget I ever said it. Whatever. It doesn't matter. Marriage or not, we are proposing to double Irwin's salary.

ISOBEL: Double it?

MARION: Yes. We did tell Irwin that.

ISOBEL: Irwin, is this true?

(IRWIN *shrugs and smiles, boyishly.*)

IRWIN: They said it.

TOM: We rate him very highly.

ISOBEL: Yes. So do I.

42

(*Her voice is very faint now. She seems dazed.*)

MARION: It does seem absurd. I couldn't believe it. Irwin says he doesn't even own his room in Kentish Town.

IRWIN: No, I don't.

MARION: At his age, really, Isobel, that is ridiculous. For an artist of his talent.

ISOBEL: Oh, yes.

(*Now she is staring at* IRWIN, *her mind miles away, as if trying to work something out.* MARION *takes a few paces, almost talking to herself.*)

MARION: If someone comes along, says, 'Look, you'll do exactly the same job, in the same hours, in the same way, the only difference is, you'll be paid double . . .' (*She smiles to herself.*) You can't blame Irwin.

RHONDA: Why do people think it's smart to be poor?

(*There's a silence, full of sadness.* MARION *frowns, surprised by* RHONDA's *sudden interruption. Then* TOM *breaks the mood, snapping his briefcase shut.*)

TOM: I have to go. I've got a total immersion at six. Are you coming with me, darling?

MARION: Yes. Rhonda's coming as well. Let's make some tea. Katherine?

KATHERINE: Oh, yes.

(*She gets up from her seat.* TOM *and* RHONDA *go first as* MARION *stops a moment at the door.*)

MARION: Think about it anyway.

(*She puts her arm round* KATHERINE *as they turn to go out.* ISOBEL *and* IRWIN *are left alone in the empty room.* ISOBEL *is turned away from him, he behind her.*)

IRWIN: Isobel, please. Just look at me. Please.

(*She doesn't turn.*)

Things move on. You brought in Katherine. Be fair, it was you. It changed the nature of the firm. For better or worse. But it's changed. And you did it. Not me.

(*There is silence.*)

I wouldn't hurt you. You know that. I'd rather die than see you hurt. I love you. I want you. There's not a moment when I don't want you.

43

(ISOBEL *stands quite still, not turning. The sound of the guns.*)

ISOBEL: The guns are getting nearer. God, will nobody leave us in peace?

(*The lights fade.*)

ACT TWO

SCENE FIVE

Isobel's new offices in the West End. The draughtsmen's desks are noticeably newer and smarter than the old ones; there are more of them stretching away into the distance towards a back wall which is dominated by a large-scale, chic, designer motif. There are pools of light fashionably formed over each desk, but for the moment only one area is occupied. IRWIN *is sitting at his board, looking down at* RHONDA *who is on a rug on the floor. She is dressed only in a short blue silk dressing gown. There is a glass of champagne at her side, and* IRWIN *has another. The place is deserted but for them. It's late.*

IRWIN: What did he do then?

RHONDA: Who?

IRWIN: This man of yours.

RHONDA: Oh, well, of course. He was ready for the pounce.

IRWIN: What was the pounce like?

RHONDA: As you'd expect. It was crude.

(She smiles.)

IRWIN: No, tell me.

RHONDA: He's a senior Tory politician. He's a Minister. Right? So he starts to talk all about his wife . . .

IRWIN: What, she doesn't understand him?

RHONDA: Uh-huh, worse than that.

IRWIN: Worse? What?

RHONDA: Guess. What's the worst thing of all?

*(*IRWIN *shrugs.)*

IRWIN: You've lost me.

RHONDA: You must have guessed.

IRWIN: No.

RHONDA: She can't come.

(Now IRWIN *smiles.)*

IRWIN: Good Lord, you astonish me. I'm trying to work out which one it must be. A Tory politician whose wife can't come.

RHONDA: Have you got it yet?

IRWIN: Not really. To be honest, I'm spoilt for choice.

RHONDA: Yeah, the thing is . . . (*She gets up. As she does, her dressing-gown falls open and shows a lot of bare leg.*) Whoops . . .

(*She passes his desk to get the bottle of champagne which is just beyond him. As she passes, he looks on the point of reaching out to her. But she gets the bottle and stands behind him, filling his glass up.*)

What are you smiling at?

IRWIN: Nothing.

RHONDA: Just keep yourself nice.

(*He smiles up at her a moment.*)

IRWIN: Yes, I will.

(*She goes to settle on the floor again with the bottle.*)

Tell me more.

RHONDA: Yeah, well, he's saying she's had some sort of accident. Ten years ago. A black man jumped out of an alley . . .

IRWIN: I see – what – and this has permanently damaged . . .

RHONDA: Look, I don't believe it any more than you. A man is talking. Do you believe anything any man says? Especially on this subject? Do you have any idea what being a woman is like? By nightfall you're stuffed. You've spent the whole day sitting listening to men deceive themselves. If you're lucky. That's if they're not actually out deceiving you.

(IRWIN *smiles, unworried.*)

IRWIN: Oh, really?

RHONDA: Anyway, this man has spotted me in the Library at the House of Commons, researching for Marion . . .

IRWIN: And what's attracted him?

(RHONDA *laughs, suddenly embarrassed.*)

RHONDA: No, I can't say.

IRWIN: No, come on, I'll tell you mine.

RHONDA: Your what?

IRWIN: My most ridiculous sexual experience.

(*She looks at him a moment. Then tells.*)

RHONDA: He saw me eating a prawn and mayonnaise sandwich. He says with my mouth half-open. So he could half see it. And this has simply driven him mad. (*She looks inquiringly at* IRWIN.) Well? Have you got him yet?

IRWIN: Agriculture and Fisheries?

RHONDA: No.

IRWIN: Is he in Defence? It's not . . .

RHONDA: No, you're nowhere near.

(*They smile.*)

I said, well, if he bought me another identical sandwich, I'd be willing to go round and eat it in his flat.

IRWIN: And did he?

(RHONDA *smiles and gathers the folds of her robe, tucking them tightly round her legs.*)

RHONDA: Why should I tell you? Isn't it more fun if you have to imagine?

IRWIN: And is that the point of this? Fun?

(*A pause.* RHONDA *looks down. Then she resumes decisively.*)

RHONDA: Also, of course, he's fanatical about secrecy. So this makes him also, not only lascivious, not only a palpable scuzzbag as you might say, but also very security-conscious. He's worried sick about where and when we're going to meet.

IRWIN: Do you meet?

RHONDA: Yes. Eventually.

IRWIN: And?

(*She pauses a moment, thoughtful.*)

RHONDA: It's the usual stuff. I don't know what he wants. Nor does he. He's like a man, that's all I can say. He's so out of touch with his feelings that he's like some great half-dead animal that lies there, just thrashing about.

IRWIN: Mmm. (*He thinks a moment, struck by her sadness.*)
Not good.

RHONDA: No. Seldom is, though. In my experience.

IRWIN: What does that mean?

RHONDA: It means men are cunt-struck. But they rarely know why.

(*There is a silence.* IRWIN *sips champagne.*)

IRWIN: Do you think that?

RHONDA: Well, I do really.

IRWIN: Is it always true?

RHONDA: Not always. Often. I find men cry out. I don't know

47

why. 'Oh, no,' they say. Like they're shocked by what they feel.

IRWIN: Good Lord. You make it sound sad.

(*There is a moment's silence.* RHONDA *looks away.*)

Have you been back?

RHONDA: Where?

IRWIN: No, I mean, with the politician?

RHONDA: Oh, you're joking. He calls. He calls all the time.

IRWIN: Do you answer?

RHONDA: One day I'm going to give him a shock. I'll get Marion to take it. And that'll be the end. (*She smiles.*) I already told her about him.

IRWIN: You told Marion?

RHONDA: Certainly. We laughed ourselves silly.

IRWIN: Goodness. *Marion?*

RHONDA: Yes. She loves gossip. Perhaps because her own life's so dull. I think that's why she employed me. She likes the idea . . .

(*But she stops in mid-sentence.*)

IRWIN: What?

RHONDA: No.

IRWIN: What are you saying?

RHONDA: She likes the idea that I cause chaos.

(*There's a pause.*)

IRWIN: And do you?

RHONDA: Not always. Sometimes I do. (*She looks at him.*) Tell me yours.

IRWIN: What?

RHONDA: Don't you have a story?

IRWIN: Oh. Not really.

RHONDA: You said you did.

IRWIN: Not at the moment. But somehow I feel I'm just about to.

RHONDA: Oh, really? Why?

(*They look at each other now.*)

IRWIN: You used a dirty word. It excited me.

RHONDA: What word?

IRWIN: Chaos.

(*There's a silence. Then* RHONDA *smiles.*)

RHONDA: Yes, I've noticed. It has an effect.

(*The door opens at the back.* ISOBEL *stands in the doorway. She is harassed, tired, carrying a soft overnight bag and a big design portfolio. Seeing* RHONDA *and* IRWIN, *she stands in the doorway, not moving.*)

IRWIN: Isobel. My goodness.

RHONDA: Good evening.

(RHONDA *quickly gets up from the floor, guiltily.* ISOBEL *puts the bags down and closes the door.*)

IRWIN: What happened to Glasgow?

ISOBEL: It was called off. (*She has moved into the room now and dumps the portfolio on his desk.*) Here, take this. It's yours. I won't be needing it. It's the industrial logo.

IRWIN: What happened?

ISOBEL: I missed the last plane.

IRWIN: But you set off hours ago.

(*Both* RHONDA *and* IRWIN *are standing, not moving, while* ISOBEL *keeps up a chain of action, collecting a pile of written messages from a pigeonhole, going to her own desk, sitting down to read them.*)

ISOBEL: Have you dealt with these messages?

IRWIN: Rhonda came round. To see our new premises.

ISOBEL: Ah.

RHONDA: I think they're great. Irwin said you even had an en-suite executive bathroom. We were talking on the phone . . .

IRWIN: Yes . . .

RHONDA: I mentioned my water was off. He said you had a new shower. I couldn't resist it.

ISOBEL: Was it good?

RHONDA: Oh. I haven't had it yet.

(*She walks across the room to the bathroom.* ISOBEL *now carries on working, opening her diary, ticking off items on lists.*)

I'm just about to.

ISOBEL: (*To* IRWIN) Did you do the layout for the publisher's ad?

IRWIN: It's here.

RHONDA: I can't wait. I hear there's a bidet.

ISOBEL: There's no bidet. There's everything else. But if that's

49

what you need you can always do handstands in the shower.

(RHONDA *stands a moment in the doorway, taking in this remark*.)

RHONDA: (*Quietly*) I'll be back in a mo.

(RHONDA *goes out.* IRWIN *is already holding the ad in his hand, and now very quietly he walks over to* ISOBEL'*s desk and slips it in front of her, then stands waiting, like an expensive butler*.)

ISOBEL: It's good.

IRWIN: Thank you. (*He waits a moment*.) I sometimes wonder . . . I don't know . . . whether you still care about my drawing.

ISOBEL: I've said I like it.

IRWIN: It hurts me. You don't always seem as if it means what it did. I draw for you. That's why I draw. To please you. To earn your good opinion. Which to me means everything.

ISOBEL: Well, you have it. So you're all right.

(*She is steady and quiet, still working.* IRWIN *moves away*.)

IRWIN: I've just been talking to Rhonda.

ISOBEL: Uh-huh.

IRWIN: I rather underestimated her. She's actually a quite interesting girl.

ISOBEL: Yes, I'm sure.

IRWIN: She has a first-class degree in economics.

(ISOBEL *has no answer to this.* IRWIN *shifts feet*.)

I mean I'm sure you probably think she's shallow . . .

ISOBEL: No. Actually, I don't. I don't think anything. Why is everyone always so eager to tell me what I think?

IRWIN: Isobel . . .

ISOBEL: I don't have an opinion. I have no opinion on the subject of Rhonda. I am absolutely neutral.

IRWIN: No, I just felt . . . from the way you greeted her . . .

(ISOBEL *turns suddenly, quite savage*.)

ISOBEL: *What?*

(IRWIN *shrugs*.)

IRWIN: Well, I think she seemed a bit put out.

ISOBEL: You felt that? And you also felt that this was my fault?

(*She is looking at him now, her anger low and dangerous*.)

IRWIN: Isobel, you know I've been meaning to talk to you. You've not been looking too well.

ISOBEL: No, that's true. I look like hell.

IRWIN: I'm worried for you.

ISOBEL: Oh, really?

(IRWIN *is quiet*.)

IRWIN: Why do you turn all my concern away?

(ISOBEL *carries on working, trying not to let any feeling she has show*.)

Look, you know I can tell when you're really angry . . .

ISOBEL: Oh, I see. Now I'm being told that I'm angry.

IRWIN: Well, you are.

ISOBEL: No, I'm not. I'm actually stopping myself. On the grounds that it would be counter-productive. I can see it's what you want. That I should get angry. But I am refusing to. And because today has been unspeakable, I am now going to go home.

(*She has got up and gone to another desk where she collects a diary, and some cosmetics*.)

IRWIN: What are you getting? Those are Katherine's things. What's happened?

(ISOBEL *turns and looks at him*.)

ISOBEL: Do you really want to know? Why not just . . .

IRWIN: Yes?

ISOBEL: Continue whatever it is you were doing.

IRWIN: I was working.

ISOBEL: Good. Then continue working.

(RHONDA *calls from the shower, loudly*.)

RHONDA: (*Off*) Is there any soap?

ISOBEL: Do your work with the soap, Irwin. And I shall go home.

IRWIN: Isobel. Where's Katherine?

(ISOBEL, *who is once more about to leave, is suddenly stopped now*.)

Why don't you tell me? I don't get it. What's going on?

(ISOBEL *turns reluctantly and looks at him a moment*.)

ISOBEL: She's in a clinic. That's where I've been. They called me at Heathrow and I came back into town. I had to get her admitted.

IRWIN: What happened?

ISOBEL: A whole lot of stuff. Some joker gave her a drink. (*She nods*.) She'd taken out those clients . . .

IRWIN: Is that the video company?

ISOBEL: Yes. It was stupid. I should have gone with her. They were unbelievably important. Over dinner they said they'd decided against our submission. So Katherine picked up a steak knife and plunged it straight for the managing director's heart.

IRWIN: My God!

ISOBEL: It's fine. It's not a problem. He's an ad-man. His heart presents a very small target. He's got a few cut ribs. And Katherine was already too drunk to take aim.

(IRWIN *looks down.*)

IRWIN: Oh shit, I'm sorry.

ISOBEL: You don't have to be sorry. It's not your fault. How often did you tell me? It was my decision. I employed her.

IRWIN: So what will you do?

ISOBEL: What can I do? We actually needed these people. They were good business. We're grossly over-extended. Look at this place! (*She gestures round the room.*) Instead . . . tonight we have a lawsuit. No, Katherine has a lawsuit. Mercifully she's under sedation. She'll wake up in the morning. And then I will face all her problems again. (*She smiles and turns to go, picking up her bag.*) Will you lock up after you?

IRWIN: Isobel!

ISOBEL: What?

IRWIN: You can't just leave now.

ISOBEL: Why not?

IRWIN: I want to talk. I'd like to help you.

(*She smiles at him generously, then goes over and touches his arm.*)

ISOBEL: I'm grateful for that. Honestly. But if you really want to help, best thing is to let me sleep.

(*He looks down, miserable.*)

IRWIN: I've got to talk.

ISOBEL: Why?

IRWIN: I need it.

ISOBEL: What, you all night and Katherine in the morning? (*The remark slips out. She at once looks down, contrite, apologetic, quiet.*) Please let me go, I've got problems enough.

IRWIN: That isn't fair.

ISOBEL: No, it isn't. I only say it because I'm tired. That's why I want to go. Please? Is that unreasonable? I want to go because I've no fairness left.

(*But* IRWIN *is still looking at her pleadingly.*)

IRWIN: Isobel, you've started avoiding me. You tolerate me, yes. But every time I look at you now, you look the other way.

ISOBEL: I'm sorry. Yes.

IRWIN: Why do you do that?

ISOBEL: I don't know. (*She smiles.*) I suppose a mistaken idea of kindness.

IRWIN: It isn't kind to avoid me.

ISOBEL: No.

IRWIN: Perhaps it's more like cowardice.

ISOBEL: Yes. (*She looks at him almost absently, smiling again.*) Shall we leave it at that?

IRWIN: I won't leave it at that.

ISOBEL: Look, all right . . . (*She is suddenly vehement as if finally accepting that she cannot avoid this argument.*) I don't understand. What do you *want* from me? Like for instance tonight. I come in. What's in the air? A smell of cheap sex . . .

IRWIN: No!

ISOBEL: And I think, oh yes, I see, I know what this is for. This is to make me into the one who's responsible. There is no purpose to this except to make me feel awful. Because I'm the girl who can't be giving this man all the love he needs.

IRWIN: I never said that.

ISOBEL: You didn't need to. All I had to do was walk in the door and I was handed a role. My role is: the woman betrayed. Well, Irwin, I don't want to play it. I've no interest in playing it. Because it's humiliating. All I get to do is make catty remarks.

(IRWIN *protests, outraged.*)

IRWIN: You're way off, we were just talking . . .

ISOBEL: The next thing, you mention I'm looking terrible. Do you know how shabby that particular remark always is? You destroy a woman's confidence, then you say, I'm so worried

53

about you, darling, you just don't seem to be yourself. Well, no. I'm not myself. I'm being turned into a person whose only function is to suffer. And believe me, it bores me just as much as it bores you.

(IRWIN *is shaking his head.*)

IRWIN: I can't believe this. How long have you been thinking this?

ISOBEL: Please don't be innocent. We've both been aware of it. You as much as me. We should have parted some months ago. We should have parted . . .

(*She stops.*)

IRWIN: When?

ISOBEL: You know when.

(*He suddenly points at her.*)

IRWIN: It still annoys you, doesn't it? That I talked to Marion and agreed to the restructuring.

ISOBEL: No. It doesn't annoy me. It's just . . .

(*She stops again.*)

IRWIN: What? Go on, please. You must say.

ISOBEL: Oh God, I can't explain. Don't you understand? It's why I never talk to you. It's why I never look at you. I can't find a way of describing what's happened, without seeming to be disgustingly cruel. (*She looks at him, suddenly assertive.*) There we are, you see, now I look at you, you're flinching already . . .

IRWIN: Isobel . . .

ISOBEL: And I'm standing here thinking, this is just stupid, I'm no longer in love with you. Why don't I just give you the push?

IRWIN: Is that what you want?

ISOBEL: Why don't I just tell you to leave? As any sensible girl would. Why? Because, actually, there's a good part of me which is very fond of you. And wants to work with you. And hold on to what is best in you. (*She is suddenly gentle again, looking at him with affection.*) So the fact is, I find it very hard.

(IRWIN *looks down, moved.*)

IRWIN: I love you.

ISOBEL: I know. I know you love me. God knows, you say it often
enough.

(*She stops him before he can protest.*)

I don't say that to be cruel. But I never hear the words without
sensing something's being asked of me. The words drain me.
From your lips they've become a kind of blackmail. They
mean, I love you and *so* . . . *So* I am entitled to be endlessly
comforted and supported and cheered . . . (*She smiles.*) Oh,
yes, and I've been happy to do it. I comforted. I supported. I
cheered. Because I got something back. But it's gone. (*She
shrugs slightly.*) We both know it. Yet you want some period in
which we both flounder together. Hang on tight while we get
sad. But I don't want to be sad. No one can remember now,
but the big joke is, by temperament I'm actually an extremely
cheerful girl. That's what's so silly. I'm strong. You sap my
strength. Because you make me feel guilty. I can never love
you as much as you need. Now I see that. So I've done a great
deal of suffering. But that's over. I'm ready to move on.

(IRWIN *is looking at her disbelievingly.*)

IRWIN: I don't believe you.

ISOBEL: You do. You do actually.

IRWIN: It's all because I failed some stupid sort of test . . .

ISOBEL: No.

IRWIN: I wasn't *loyal*. I talked to your sister.

ISOBEL: That's nothing to do with it.

IRWIN: Yes, it is. That was my crime.

(ISOBEL *tries to interrupt.*)

ISOBEL: No, you're wrong. It's not that. It's just . . . I had an idea
of you . . .

IRWIN: I know that idea. You saw me as poor and under your spell.
As soon as I looked round and said, 'Hold on, this is
ridiculous, please may I now have a living wage?' then . . . *then*
of course you didn't like it. Because I was no longer in thrall.
To the lady of the manor. I'm not under your patronage.

ISOBEL: Good. (*She smiles.*) Then you have what you want.

IRWIN: No. (*He is quiet.*) I want you.

ISOBEL: *Why*, for God's sake, if I'm what you say I am, if I'm –
what? – patronizing . . .

IRWIN: No . . .

ISOBEL: If I'm – what then? – possessive of you, if I'm this terrible influence, then plainly you're better off free of me.

IRWIN: No. That's not right.

(*He looks her straight in the eye, suddenly calm and strong, as if knowing he has a strong hand to play.*)

I'm still in love with you. I always will be. There's nothing I can do. It's just . . . (*He pauses.*) It's time you faced up to some truths.

(ISOBEL *is quiet, mistrustful, as if fearing what will be said.*)

ISOBEL: What truths?

IRWIN: It's hurt me to watch you. Lately. You know very well. You must change.

ISOBEL: How?

IRWIN: You must grow up. You have this crazy idea of integrity.

ISOBEL: Crazy?

IRWIN: Yes. You have this idea because your father was a failure, because he sat in Gloucestershire, losing money hand over fist, but universally pleasant and kind, you think anyone who lives differently has to be some sort of traitor. You think I betrayed you. Well, don't you? (*He waits a moment.*) Not everyone can be your father, you know.

(ISOBEL *is already shaking her head.*)

ISOBEL: That's really naive. You're nowhere near it.

IRWIN: Aren't I?

ISOBEL: Of course not.

IRWIN: Then why, tell me why you will sacrifice your whole life for Katherine?

ISOBEL: Don't be ridiculous. That's not what I'm doing.

IRWIN: Isn't it?

ISOBEL: No! (*She moves away, uneasy.*) 'Sacrifice'! Irwin, really, what a word.

(*But he presses his point home, insistent.*)

IRWIN: Like tonight. The knife business. Did you notice? She reserves it for the big contract. She doesn't flash a knife for the little guys, you know. She has priorities. She waits for the really major customer. With a great deal of money. Which we desperately need. Then . . . *then* she gives us a glimpse of her act.

(ISOBEL *turns to him, panicking slightly.*)

ISOBEL: What are you saying?

IRWIN: I'm saying, look, like right now, her head is on a nice white pillow in a hospital – where?

ISOBEL: North London.

IRWIN: All right. Now if at this moment we did a brainscan, tell me, what do you think we would see?

ISOBEL: I don't know.

IRWIN: *What?*

(ISOBEL *shifts again, unhappy.*)

ISOBEL: Vapours. Alcohol. Confusion. Loss. I don't know. (*Suddenly she shouts.*) *I don't know.*

IRWIN: Yes, you do.

(*There's a silence.*)

Isobel, she's dreaming of ways to destroy you.

ISOBEL: No.

IRWIN: Yes.

ISOBEL: Don't be absurd. You mustn't say that.

IRWIN: Why not? Just tell me. What state was your father in when he died? He'd had the life beaten out of him.

ISOBEL: No.

IRWIN: I know, you think she's just unhappy. She's maladjusted. She hates herself. Well, she does. And she is. All these things are true. But also it's true, Isobel, my dear, you must learn something else. That everyone knows except you. It's time you were told. There's such a thing as evil. You're dealing with evil.

(ISOBEL *turns round, about to speak.*)

That's right. And if you don't admit it, then you can't fight it. And if you don't fight it, you're going to lose.

(*There's a moment's silence. Then* RHONDA *comes through from the bathroom. She is now fully clothed in a smart skirt and pullover, her hair still wet from the shower. She is cheerful.*)

RHONDA: That was great. This place is a major achievement.

IRWIN: Ah, good.

RHONDA: I don't know how anyone ever has baths.

IRWIN: No.

RHONDA: Baths are disgusting. Sitting in your own dirty water.

Just lying there while the water gets muckier around you. It must be unhealthy. I think everyone should shower, don't you?

IRWIN: What?

(*He is looking at* ISOBEL, *who is standing thinking, taking no notice of* RHONDA.)

Oh, yes.

RHONDA: Well, anyway, I'm going to the flicks. Excuse me.

ISOBEL: We'll come with you.

RHONDA: I'm sorry?

ISOBEL: I'd like to come.

(IRWIN *looks across amazed*, RHONDA *puzzled*.)

RHONDA: It's very violent. I saw the trailer. It's one of those Los Angeles crime things. Rooms full of blood. Then the cop says, 'Right, I want everyone here to help look for his ear . . .'

ISOBEL: Sounds fine. My car's outside.

(*She turns and looks at* IRWIN.)

IRWIN: Let's have a big bag of popcorn. Then we can have a good time.

(*Before they can leave, we hear the sound of* MARION'*s voice as she approaches from the back. The scenery changes as the others leave, and we are in Tom's office – an anonymously decorated room of glass and wood panel, dominated by a big, bare leather-topped desk. The glass runs unnaturally high, giving a feeling of airy emptiness.* TOM *is already at his desk to greet his wife, who approaches, putting down her coat as she comes.*)

SCENE SIX

Tom's office.

MARION: I can't see the problem. There really is no problem. People so love to talk problems up. Family things actually belong at the weekend. A drink on Sunday is lovely. Or lunch. Or walking after lunch. That's the right time for the

58

family. It's crazy when it starts infecting your week.
(TOM *gets up from behind the desk. He is nervous.* MARION *sits down, impatient.*)

TOM: I'm sorry. I can't help it. I'm worried.

MARION: Why be worried?

TOM: They may be angry.

MARION: There's no point in being angry. They know you already own the firm. It's simply an administrative decision. Which makes total economic sense.

TOM: To you. To me also. I'm just hoping they will see it that way.
(*At once* IRWIN *appears at the door. He is subtly changed. He is glossier, better dressed, more outwardly confident in a grey and white herringbone coat and cashmere scarf. He stands a moment, saying nothing.*)
Oh, Irwin, it's you.

IRWIN: Yes.

MARION: Where's Isobel?

IRWIN: I don't know. Isn't she here?

TOM: Why, no.

MARION: We thought she was with you.

IRWIN: No. I haven't seen her.
(*There is an uneasy silence, no one moving.*)
You wanted a board meeeting?

TOM: Yes.
(IRWIN *smiles and spreads his hands.*)

IRWIN: Here I am.

TOM: You look very well.
(*There is a pause.*)

IRWIN: Look, to be honest, I think we might as well begin.

TOM: Oh, really?

IRWIN: Yes. Isobel isn't around much.

MARION: I see.

IRWIN: No.

TOM: Who's been running the business?

IRWIN: I have.

MARION: What, on your own?

IRWIN: More or less, yes.

(*There's a silence.*)

MARION: We did hear a rumour. We heard that you'd parted.

(IRWIN *just looks at her.*)

What a stupid girl.

TOM: I'm sorry . . .

IRWIN: No, it's fine.

MARION: We did hear that.

TOM: But surely it shouldn't affect the running of the firm?

(*Before* IRWIN *can answer* MARION *interrupts.*)

MARION: What happened?

IRWIN: Well . . .

MARION: Rhonda did tell us something . . .

(IRWIN *takes a quick look to* MARION, *taking this in.*)

IRWIN: Of course she was there. We all went to the cinema.
During the film, I looked round and she'd gone. I assumed
to the ladies room. Or to buy popcorn. What can I say? It
was terribly embarrassing. I mean, explaining to Rhonda.
(*He looks down.*) Isobel went and she never came back.

MARION: When was this?

IRWIN: Three weeks ago. In fact it turned out she'd gone straight
to Heathrow. Got the first plane at dawn and left the
country.

(TOM *frowns.*)

TOM: Goodness me.

MARION: But she's back now?

IRWIN: Oh, yes. She came back quite quickly.

MARION: She's looking after Katherine.

IRWIN: Yes. She's living there. She also bought back your dad's
house.

MARION: It's deplorable.

IRWIN: It was the first thing she did. She stopped the sale going
through. Katherine was going to use the money to buy a flat.
Well, Isobel's going to buy a flat for her. The one thing,
however, she hasn't done . . .

(*He stops, suddenly overcome, as if about to cry.*)

TOM: Are you all right?

IRWIN: (*Nods*) Well, anyway, we don't see her at work. (*He stares
ahead a moment.*) So.

TOM: I'm sorry, Irwin.

MARION: It's so typical, isn't it? She's feckless. She was born irresponsible. Someone said, 'Do you know what politics is? Finally? Politics is being there every day.' And you know it's true. You have to be there. I'm there every day. Aren't I, darling?

TOM: You are.

MARION: And I'm there the next day. And the next day. And the next day. For ever. Isn't that right?

TOM: Well, yes . . .

(*He stops, embarrassed.*)

MARION: What?

TOM: No, I mean, at least, I was going to say . . . at least till you die.

MARION: Of course. Why say that? That goes without saying.

TOM: Yes. No, you're right. I was just . . . pointing it out.

(*But* MARION *has already moved on.*)

MARION: But, Isobel, oh no, if there's trouble, straightaway, 'I can't face it,' she says . . .

TOM: Well . . .

MARION: 'I've had a little tiff with my boyfriend.' Soon as that happens it's upsticks and a wave and, 'Oh, off I go.' She's totally unfocused. (*She leans forward in her chair.*) Did you hear what happened before the funeral?

IRWIN: No.

TOM: I'm not sure . . .

MARION: After Dad died? Actually in the room Dad was lying in? She asked Tom to spy on me.

TOM: Darling . . .

MARION: It's true. You told me. She actually took Tom aside and said, 'Does Marion hate me?' It's *true*. 'If she does will you promise to tell me?' She asked Tom! Really! Is this the act of a normal, well-adjusted person? Please. Spare me. All my life I've had people say, 'Oh, she's the nice one.' (MARION *sits back.*) Nice? I think I call that paranoid, don't you?

(IRWIN *looks down, embarrassed.*)

IRWIN: It's very difficult. You see, since she got back, Isobel won't speak to me.

(MARION *is immediately triumphant*.)

MARION: Well, pardon me, I think that says it all. Let's face it, we've all been through it, we've all known people we've been fond of . . . (*She casts a reassuring glance*.) Before I was married, of course . . . I mean, however badly it ends, you don't just not speak to them. Do you? Is that normal? Please! We've all had our hearts broken. But really! (*She shakes her head*.) I'm sorry to say this. I wouldn't say it unless I were seriously concerned. But I think we should be considering professional help.

TOM: Marion . . .

MARION: I do. I've said it. I'm sorry. Get someone in who's experienced. These days there's no stigma attached. As far as I'm concerned, it's like fixing a car. If it breaks, just mend it. It's all avoidable. Nowadays they have brilliant people.
(IRWIN *is looking down*.)

IRWIN: I'm not sure things are quite at that stage. It's more . . . (*He stops*.)

TOM: What?

IRWIN: She's my whole life. I'm still in love with her. I know I sound ridiculous.

TOM: No. Not at all.

IRWIN: What do you do? When everything you think, everything you feel is screaming at you that you belong with her?
(*He looks up*.)
What do I know? Very little. A bit about drawing. A bit about how to look after myself. Which I've done for years. Beyond that, nothing. Except I've known one certain source of good.
(TOM *is looking at him closely*.)
And now I've lost it. It's gone.
(TOM *is puzzled, worried*.)

TOM: But what about work? Today, I mean, we have a crucial decision. We've had an excellent approach. We're being offered twice what we paid for the premises. It's a very good offer. We need to respond to it.

IRWIN: I'm afraid she seems to have no interest in the firm.

TOM: It's extraordinary.

IRWIN: No, not really. It's all of a piece. While I work there, I don't think she's going to come near it. *(He smiles sourly.)* My guess is she's made some sort of vow.
> *(The phone rings.* TOM *answers it on his desk.* MARION *is extremely provoked by what* IRWIN *has said.)*

TOM: Yes?

MARION: I don't believe this. This is most peculiar. What is this? A *vow*? It's outrageous. People making *vows*. What are *vows*? Nobody's made vows since the nineteenth century.
> *(*TOM *holds his hand over the phone.)*

TOM: It's Isobel.

MARION: Well?

TOM: She's downstairs. She says she won't come up until Irwin leaves.
> *(There's a moment's pause only. Then* IRWIN *gets up from his chair and picks up his scarf to put round his neck.)*

MARION: No, Irwin, please. I forbid you to go. This is ridiculous.

TOM: What do I tell her?

IRWIN: Tell her I'm leaving.
> *(*TOM *speaks into the phone.)*

TOM: He says he's going. It's all right. There are two exits.
> *(*TOM *smiles as he puts the phone down.)*

MARION: This is absurd. I will not have this.

IRWIN: Will you put your proposal in writing?

TOM: Of course.
> *(*IRWIN *nods at* MARION.*)*

IRWIN: Marion. Excuse me. I don't want a scene.

TOM: Any messages?

IRWIN: No. No, thank you, Tom.
> *(He walks across and shakes his hand.* TOM *puts his hand on his arm.)*

TOM: You're shaking.

IRWIN: No. I'm just cold.
> *(He turns and goes out. There is a moment's silence as* MARION *sits, genuinely angry.* TOM *looks away. Suddenly she speaks, the anger high in her now.)*

MARION: We live in this world. We try to make a living. Most of us just try to get on with our lives. Why can't we?

TOM: I don't know.

MARION: Why does there have to be this endless complication?

(ISOBEL *has appeared in the other doorway. She is also changed. She wears a long dark blue overcoat and thin glasses. Her hair is swept back on her head. She appears tense, thin, but also strangely cheerful.*)

Isobel.

(*At once* ISOBEL *comes warmly across the room, smiling and embracing* MARION *when she reaches her.*)

ISOBEL: Marion. Hello. How are you? I've missed you terribly.

TOM: Hello.

ISOBEL: Tom. How are you? (*She goes over to kiss him.*) It's such a lovely day out there. It's incredible. I've never seen the sun so high at this time of year. It's beautiful. I've spent half an hour in the park. Have you seen?

TOM: No.

MARION: No, actually. We've been too busy.

ISOBEL: I'm sure.

MARION: I'd love to spend my day just staring at the sun.

(ISOBEL *catches her tone, but tries to ignore it, keeping cheerful.*)

ISOBEL: I've never been here. What a nice office!

MARION: Isobel. Please.

ISOBEL: Yes?

MARION: Could you just tell us what's going on?

(ISOBEL *smiles at* MARION, *who is looking at her unforgivingly.*)

ISOBEL: Of course. I'm sorry we can't have a proper board meeting. At the moment it's difficult between Irwin and me. It'll get better.

MARION: Now listen . . .

ISOBEL: Forgive me, I don't want to talk about it. Shall we talk about business?

(*She smiles cheerfully at* TOM *trying to make interruption impossible.*)

TOM: Of course.

(ISOBEL *is suddenly decisive.*)

ISOBEL: You want to sell the firm because it's not profitable and sack all the staff, is that right?

MARION: (*Rising at once*) Now that isn't fair.

64

ISOBEL: Please. I'm not judging. Marion, I'm just asking the
facts.

(ISOBEL *sits opposite* TOM *at the desk.*)

We redecorated the premises you bought us. They're now
commercially very attractive. You can make a profit by
selling them. You can double your money. But then of
course there's nowhere for us to go.

TOM: That isn't quite it. (*He smiles.*) There is also the point you
are losing money. Sadly, the expansion hasn't really worked.

ISOBEL: Well, no. I did warn you.

TOM: I mean, any responsible businessman would tell you at this
point he has a duty to his own survival. We have no real
choice. We have to get out.

(ISOBEL *smiles.*)

ISOBEL: With a little profit?

TOM: Well, certainly.

ISOBEL: Is it true we didn't cost anything in the first place?

MARION: Isobel . . .

(*But* ISOBEL, *who is quite calm and gentle, puts up her hand to
stop* MARION's *indignant interruptions.*)

ISOBEL: Look, I'm just asking. Someone said you wrote us off
against tax. Is that right?

(*She has to put her hand up again to quell the next interruption.*)

Marion, please. I'm not criticizing. Is it true, because of tax,
we cost you nothing?

TOM: In a sense.

MARION: Why apologize?

ISOBEL: No, I don't expect it.

TOM: It is legitimate business practice.

ISOBEL: Of course.

(*She smiles a moment at* MARION, *calming her down.*)

And now I imagine your tax position has changed.

TOM: Exactly.

ISOBEL: Selling is now advantageous.

TOM: Yes, that's right.

ISOBEL: And the extra workers we took on?

TOM: They would be compensated.

ISOBEL: How much?

TOM: Three weeks' wages.

    (*There's a pause, while* ISOBEL *thinks this over.*)

ISOBEL: Uh-huh.

    (*There's a silence as* ISOBEL *nods slightly, not moving. Then she sweeps her hand across Tom's desk.*)

MARION: Now, look, Isobel . . .

ISOBEL: Well, I guess that's it.

MARION: I wouldn't call them workers. Ex-students, more like. And ex- is being kind. They've had six months' fun at high wages. Now they're back on the market. I don't think they'll want to complain.

ISOBEL: No. (*She shrugs slightly.*) Then it's done.

TOM: What d'you mean? Let's be clear. Are you agreeing? (*He is disturbed at the ease of his own victory, puzzled now.*) Isobel?

ISOBEL: Why even ask me? I'm only one vote.

    (*She smiles as if that were the end of it.* MARION *is looking at her suspiciously.*)

MARION: Now listen, Isobel, what are you up to?

ISOBEL: Up to? Nothing.

MARION: You think you're being clever.

ISOBEL: Not at all.

MARION: I get the drift of your questions.

ISOBEL: They have no drift. I've simply been establishing the facts.

MARION: Oh yes, I know what you think of us.

ISOBEL: What I think? Oh, really? How?

    (ISOBEL *is half smiling.* MARION *is angry.*)

MARION: I just *know*.

ISOBEL: I don't think so. Perhaps you know what you yourself feel. But that's different.

MARION: What do you mean? (*She is panicking now.*) I've nothing on my conscience. I don't feel anything.

ISOBEL: Good. Then in that case, everything's fine. (*She looks at her a moment, then smiles.*) I must be off.

    (*She begins to get up.*)

MARION: Oh, no, you don't get away that easily . . .

ISOBEL: Tom. Goodbye.

MARION: Just tell me. What did that mean? About what *I* feel?

(ISOBEL *has walked across and taken her hands. She looks her straight in the eye, with great warmth.*)

ISOBEL: It meant nothing. Marion. Please let's be friends.

MARION: We're always friends.

ISOBEL: Good.

MARION: I have no worries. I'm fine.

(*She is abashed by* ISOBEL *standing so close to her, so friendly. But as soon as* ISOBEL *turns, she speaks again.*)

It's not *me*, I'm just concerned for Irwin.

ISOBEL: Irwin?

MARION: Yes.

ISOBEL: Why, what did he say?

(TOM *looks uneasily to* MARION.)

TOM: Now, Marion, please . . .

MARION: It's none of my business. I'm just telling you, as an impartial observer. You're being very selfish.

ISOBEL: I see.

MARION: It's a fact. If you won't go in to work, then, let's be sensible, there's no future for the firm. In sheer business terms. It happens to need both of you.

ISOBEL: Marion, you heard Tom. The firm has no future anyway.

TOM: Good gracious, no, excuse me, I didn't say that. Not at all. I'm hoping the two of you are going to continue.

(ISOBEL *turns, bewildered, for the first time slightly raising her voice.*)

ISOBEL: But, Tom, you just said, we've got nowhere to go.

TOM: Actually, there is a place. In this very building. It's a stroke of luck. I was getting round to saying. Did you happen to come through the car park?

ISOBEL: I did.

TOM: Well, probably you saw it. It's over there.

(*There's a pause.*)

ISOBEL: Ah, yes.

TOM: It's ideal. It's there. It's available. It's a base if you want one.

ISOBEL: I see.

(*She is just staring at him. He is waiting a moment.*)

TOM: We could let you have it rent-free. We'd pay your heat and lighting for a year, say. I mean for nothing. We'd throw it in. Absolutely free. As a pure favour. Gratis.

ISOBEL: Well, thank you. (*She is looking across the desk at him. Now she speaks very quietly.*) But as I'm not with Irwin, it doesn't arise.

TOM: (*Smiles*) No.

MARION: Now wait, look, Isobel . . .

ISOBEL: (*To* TOM) All right?

MARION: I'm a bit shocked by this. Tom is making a very decent offer. He's giving you a chance. He's saying he'll overlook the fact that you messed up the expansion.

ISOBEL: But of course I never wanted the expansion.

MARION: Well, exactly. Isn't that the whole point? I think you deliberately sabotaged it . . .

ISOBEL: Oh, I see.

MARION: Just to make your point. And now when Tom's saying, all right, put that in the past, I'll give you a second chance, you seem determined to throw it right back in his face.
(ISOBEL *smiles, unable to avoid answering, her patience going, but still with humour.*)

ISOBEL: Well, no, I don't think so, I mean, look, I'm not complaining, whatever's happened is my own fault, I was out of my depth, no, I was weak, but putting that aside I have just been – what is the word for it? – I think I have just been *asset-stripped*. Isn't that the term for it? 'Objectively', as you would say, I have just been trashed and spat out in lumps. And now Tom has a corrugated hut at the back of his factory between, as I saw it, the car park and the waste-disposal unit on an industrial estate in Welwyn Garden City. (*She turns to* TOM.) Forgive me, but I think even Jesus might have doubts about setting up a business in there.
(*Surprisingly* TOM *chuckles at this, but* ISOBEL's *energy has unleashed all* MARION's *incoherent fury.*)

MARION: Now this is it . . .

ISOBEL: I'm sorry . . .

MARION: This is exactly it. You spoil everything you touch. Everywhere you go, there are arguments. God, how I hate all this human stuff. Wherever you go, you cause misery.

68

People crying, people not talking. It overwhelms me. Because you can't just live. Why can't you *live*, like other people? (*She stares at* ISOBEL, *distressed, in tears.*) Irwin came in here. He's in agony. He's a nice man.

ISOBEL: He is a nice man. Except to me. That's the difference. He's in the grip of an obsession. Which he can't help. He's furious because I'm no longer in love with him. He can't accept that. And because I know him very well, I'm fearful. Because in a way I think he never will.

MARION: Don't be ridiculous. He's just an ordinary person. We talked to him. He's an ordinary man.

(ISOBEL *turns, ignoring this.*)

ISOBEL: And so I decided, perhaps it's irrational, all my life I've got on with everyone. But this one time, all my instincts say, 'Do something decisive. Cut him off. Wake him up. Shock him. Make it final.' (*She turns, thoughtful now.*) 'Do what needs to be done.'

MARION: Really?

ISOBEL: Yes.

MARION: Was flying off necessary?

(ISOBEL *smiles at the memory.*)

TOM: Where did you go?

ISOBEL: I took the first plane that came. Lanzarote, as it happened.

TOM: How was that?

ISOBEL: Paradise. I took all my clothes off and walked along the beach. Lanzarote was paradise. But unfortunately no use to me. (*She laughs.*) You can't get away. You think you can. You think you'll fly out. Just leave. Damn the lot of you, and go. Then you think, here I am, stark naked, sky-blue sea, miles of sand – I've done it! I'm free! Then you think, yes, just remind me, what am I meant to do now? (*She stands, a mile away in a world of her own.*) In my case there's only one answer. (*She looks absently at them, as if they were not even present.*) I must do what Dad would have wished. (*She turns, as if this were self-evident.*) That's it.

MARION: You are insufferable. You are truly insufferable. Hide behind your father for the rest of your life. Die there!

(MARION *is suddenly screaming.* ISOBEL *looks down, undisturbed.*)

ISOBEL: Yes, well, no doubt I shall.

(*She turns and goes out.* TOM *stands appalled.*)

TOM: You went too far.

MARION: No, Tom, please . . .

TOM: I should never have done this. I didn't see what would happen. I can't believe it, I saw nothing at all. (*He looks up.*) I'm going down to pray. I fear for her.

(TOM *goes.* MARION *is left alone, astonished by* TOM's *departure.*)

MARION: Tom. Tom. Please come back.

(*At once* KATHERINE's *voice from the back as she advances towards us, the new scene replacing the old. Katherine's flat is undecorated, high-ceilinged, with peeling paintwork and cornices, a selection of lamps dotted around among old sofas and chairs. At the centre, a plain wooden table. She looks as if she has barely moved in.* KATHERINE *is in trousers and pullover, calling towards an unseen* ISOBEL.)

SCENE SEVEN

Katherine's flat.

KATHERINE: I'm not going, I tell you. I don't want to go. Why should I? What gives you the right? You're so superior. Do this. Do that. As if you always knew. You don't know. I'm not doing what you tell me. So leave it. Just leave it.

(*She sits down on a small wooden chair.* ISOBEL *comes in with a hot dish between oven gloves. She sets it down on the table.* ISOBEL *is even more distant, her hair wispy across her face, her manner detached.*)

ISOBEL: I only said it would be nice to go for a walk.

KATHERINE: Well, it wouldn't be nice.

ISOBEL: No, plainly.

KATHERINE: What's this?

ISOBEL: Shepherd's pie.
>   (KATHERINE *looks up at her.*)
KATHERINE: Are you out of your mind?
ISOBEL: Eat.
KATHERINE: Your cooking is unspeakable. It's all good
>   intentions. Fuck shepherd's pie. It sums you up.
>   (ISOBEL *takes no notice, just helps herself to some.* KATHERINE
>   *watches with distaste.*)
KATHERINE: All right, let's go out. Let's go to a French
>   restaurant.
ISOBEL: Don't be ridiculous.
KATHERINE: Why not? Why not, for God's sake?
>   (ISOBEL *does not reply.*)
>   Sell Robert's house.
ISOBEL: No.
KATHERINE: Then you'd have some money.
ISOBEL: Not much.
KATHERINE: Mortgage it.
ISOBEL: It's already mortgaged.
KATHERINE: There's nobody living there. It's just sitting there.
>   Like us. (*She turns away impatiently.*) I'd rather be a drunk.
>   Why don't you let me have a drink? At least when you drink
>   you're alive. (*She gets up.*) What's life for? Jesus! Life means
>   getting out there. Having some emotion. Is that right? When
>   I went to all those terrible AA meetings, they kept saying
>   people drink because they're angry. When you get angry,
>   they tell you, count to five before you reply. Why should I
>   count to five? It's what happens *before* you count to five
>   which makes life interesting.
>   (ISOBEL *looks at her a moment. She has been eating
>   automatically, in a trance.*)
ISOBEL: Mmm.
KATHERINE: What does that mean?
>   (ISOBEL *takes no notice.*)
>   This is the worst. This feeling we're just avoiding life. Look!
>   Look!
>   (*She snaps her fingers in front of* ISOBEL's *face but* ISOBEL *does
>   not react.*)

You won't even fight.

ISOBEL: I don't want to. (*She pauses a moment, fork in hand.*) If you ask me, then I will go.

KATHERINE: Go.

(ISOBEL *gathers up her supper, her plate, the dish, the fork, the knife, the salt, the pepper and goes out.* KATHERINE *stands a moment, not moving. Then* ISOBEL *returns, gets her big blue overcoat down from a hook, puts it on without saying anything.*) Please don't leave me. Please, Isobel. Just stay for tonight. (ISOBEL *stops a moment, then walks over to the mantelpiece where there is a packet of cigarettes. She lights one. She stands with her back to the fireplace, leaning, still in the big overcoat.* KATHERINE *speaks quietly.*)

I don't know what to do. It's all such an effort. Like at school one term I worked really hard. I came fifteenth. I thought, this is stupid. Other people come second without trying. Why has God made me so fucking mediocre? The first boyfriend I had, it was the same. I adored him. I gave myself over. I couldn't get enough of him. Then one day he just stopped sleeping with me. Bang. Just like that. No warning. It happened again, the next three boyfriends I had. I thought, oh I see, there is something about me which is actually repulsive. After a while men don't want me. (*She thinks a moment.*) Well, that feeling is hard.

(ISOBEL *just listens, smoking her cigarette, not reacting.*)

That night in the restaurant, I knew I couldn't do it. I just looked at them. I could see what they were thinking. She is not confident. I do not want to do business with her. They said, 'Oh, of course, you can't have a drink, can you?' It made me so angry. I thought, count to five. It's like they have to say it. Just to make you feel worse. So they all start drinking vodka. In these really posh surroundings. They keep drinking more. And I think, oh God, you as well. Please give me a break. Just look at me as if you trust me. As if there were a little goodness in me. Then they say, 'Well, of course, you never really thought we'd give you the contract, did you? This can hardly come as a surprise.' (*She smiles.*) What do you do? I just want to hurt them. The managing director is eating a little bird. He keeps picking little bits out of his teeth. And drinking more vodka. And laughing. He says, 'No hard feelings.' I start counting to five. I don't even get to three. I suddenly yell out, 'Yes, there fucking well are. There *are* hard feelings. Because you have all the power. And you love to exercise it. And oil it with vodka. And smile your stupid shiny smiles. And you have just ditched me, you have just landed me, right back, right back into my terrible un-confidence . . .' (*She shakes her head.*) You know what happened. I reached for a drink. A few minutes later I picked up my knife. (*She shrugs slightly and turns to* ISOBEL.) It wasn't *so* wrong. Was it? At least I was alive. Not like now.

ISOBEL: No.

KATHERINE: Living here.

ISOBEL: Mmm.

(*There is a short silence.* ISOBEL's *thoughts are unreadable. She moves.*)

I think perhaps we should both go to bed. (*She has gone to the main door.*) Look. The lock. Katherine. It's not enough. You must also put the bolt on. I told you.

KATHERINE: I know.

ISOBEL: Somehow Irwin's got a key.

KATHERINE: Well, I didn't give it to him.

(ISOBEL *looks at her a moment, not believing this.*)

ISOBEL: No. It's on. All right? Where do you want to sleep?

KATHERINE: Oh, I'll take the bedroom.

(ISOBEL *has walked across to the phone which she has now unplugged from the wall. She is just about to leave the room when* KATHERINE *speaks suddenly.*)

Isobel.

ISOBEL: What?

KATHERINE: I never know what you think. I wish I knew what you thought of me.

(*There's a silence.* ISOBEL *smiles, before leaving.*)

ISOBEL: I'll tell you one day.

(ISOBEL *goes out.* KATHERINE *does not move. Then she gets up and turns out the main light. Then she turns out a standard lamp. One small light is on only.* KATHERINE *goes to the door and undoes the bolt* ISOBEL *has just put on. She stands a moment, quite still. She is still by the door as* ISOBEL *returns, now in pyjamas with a book in her hand.*)

Help me with the bed.

(*They go to the sofa. They fold it down.* ISOBEL *throws a duvet on top.* KATHERINE *moves round to her side.* ISOBEL *looks at her a moment. Then embraces her, kissing her on the cheek.*)

KATHERINE: Good night.

(*She turns and goes out.* ISOBEL *alone. She looks a moment at the bed, but then goes and picks up a book from beside the bed. She sits down in the armchair under the one lamp. She begins to read. Almost at once there is a sound from outside the door. She gets up in panic, making a move towards the door, then turning equally fast and heading to the lamp which she now turns out. There is absolute darkness. Then the door opens.* IRWIN *stands in the lit doorway, a silhouette, as* MARION *was in the opening scene. Then he closes the door. Darkness. He clicks at the main light switch. Nothing. There is a pause.*)

IRWIN: I know you're there.

(ISOBEL *turns the lamp on. She stands quite still beside it.*)

ISOBEL: You're wrong to do this.

IRWIN: Do what?

(*Neither of them moves.*)

ISOBEL: Who let you in? I bolted the door. (*She calls through to the other room, not moving.*) Katherine! Katherine!

(*There is no noise.*)

She goes to bed with a Walkman.

IRWIN: She knows I phone you every day. She feels I've been badly treated. She wants you and me to make up.

ISOBEL: Well, that's very good of her.

(IRWIN *is very quiet.*)

IRWIN: May I just sleep with you?

ISOBEL: No.

IRWIN: Why not? Please.

ISOBEL: It's over. If you sleep with me, it'll be worse. It'll make you unhappy.

IRWIN: I can't be more unhappy.

ISOBEL: It's still better you don't.

74

(*She is looking at him fearfully, still not moving. He walks into the room, she watching.*)

I'd make you some tea, but there's no milk.

(*He has moved to the table. He takes out a small handgun and lays it on the surface.*)

What's that?

IRWIN: I bought it to kill myself.

ISOBEL: You won't kill yourself. Is it loaded? Please. Give it here.

(*She takes a couple of steps towards him. But he is still right next to the table and the gun.*)

IRWIN: You're not frightened. Why aren't you frightened?

ISOBEL: I don't know. I take what comes.

IRWIN: Then make love to me.

(*She is looking at him, very quiet. Very open, as if she has already imagined his presence.*)

ISOBEL: Force me. You can force me if you like. Why not? You can take me here. On the bed. On the floor. You can fuck me till the morning. You can fuck me all tomorrow. Then the whole week. At the end you can shoot me and hold my heart in your hand. You still won't have what you want. (*Her gaze does not wander.*) The bit that you want I'm not giving you. You can make me say or do anything you like. Sure, I'll do it. Sure, I'll say it. But you'll never have the bit that you need. It isn't yours.

IRWIN: Don't say that.

ISOBEL: It isn't.

(*There is a pause.*)

IRWIN: It's you. You've destroyed me. I don't sleep. I can't make sense of life. Everywhere I go, there's nowhere to hide. I can't rest. One day I tried to work, people said, 'Oh, where's that nice girl who used to be with you?' Now I don't even work. I'm powerless. I only want one thing. To go back. To go back to where we were.

ISOBEL: It isn't possible.

IRWIN: Why? (*He is suddenly passionate.*) All that time we were together, then once only, I do one thing, one thing which you think is wrong. That's it. I'm tipped out the window, like I'm rubbish. Because I've broken one rule. Katherine

75

breaks a thousand rules. She breaks the rules all the time. All she does is betray you, day after day. Tonight, for God's sake, who do you think let me in? And why? So she can listen to me beat you round the head. And yet you go on taking care of her. Tell me, where is the justice in that?

(ISOBEL *smiles at the phrase*.)

Well?

ISOBEL: I'm staying with Katherine. Someone has to take care of her. She has no resources. It isn't her fault. It's just a fact.

(IRWIN *is suddenly quiet*.)

IRWIN: I have no worth. I can't feel my worth. When I was with you, it was there. Now it's as if you've withdrawn your approval. And I feel worthless.

ISOBEL: I know.

IRWIN: Well?

(*He waits*.)

ISOBEL: What?

IRWIN: Why don't you help me? Come back to me.

ISOBEL: No.

(*There's a pause*.)

IRWIN: Why not?

ISOBEL: It wouldn't be honest.

IRWIN: Honest? Are you honest with her?

ISOBEL: She's different.

IRWIN: Why? I was there when she landed on you. You didn't even want her.

ISOBEL: No. She came my way. It was an accident, really. But I made a commitment. Why should I drop it just because the going gets hard?

(IRWIN *is impatient*.)

IRWIN: You could say the same about me.

ISOBEL: Yes, but you're an adult. And we were in love. And you have this idea that I can't accept.

IRWIN: What's that?

(*She looks hard at him a moment*.)

ISOBEL: You want to be saved through another person.

(*There's a silence*.)

IRWIN: And?

ISOBEL: It isn't possible.

IRWIN: Isn't it?

ISOBEL: I don't know. I don't think so. (*She pauses a moment, then she begins to move.*) Now I'm going to bed.

IRWIN: Don't move.

ISOBEL: I want you to leave.

IRWIN: I told you, don't move.

    (*He has begun to raise his voice, in panic.*)

ISOBEL: Don't *move*? Good Lord, that will make life pretty difficult.

IRWIN: Please, I'm not making a joke.

ISOBEL: Oh, really?

    (*She moves towards the table where the gun is lying. He is still standing next to it. Now he screams.*)

IRWIN: I am telling you.

    (*She stops.*)

ISOBEL: Are you threatening me? What? (*She holds her hands above her head, in a little parody. She is very quiet.*) Will you hit me?

IRWIN: Isobel, please, don't make me . . .

    (*He stops, ashamed.*)

ISOBEL: What? Make you what, Irwin?

    (*He looks down, not able to answer.*)

    No, please tell me. Go on.

IRWIN: No, nothing.

ISOBEL: Please say.

    (*He looks down, not able to answer.*)

    If you kill me, will that be my fault as well?

    (*At once* KATHERINE *comes in from the bedroom. She is fully dressed, now taking in the scene between them, but not yet seeing the gun on the table.*)

IRWIN: Katherine . . .

KATHERINE: Oh, shit. I heard something.

ISOBEL: Irwin, are you going to leave?

IRWIN: Not just now.

ISOBEL: Then I'm sorry. Katherine, can you get the police?

    (ISOBEL *is capable, clear.* KATHERINE *frowns.*)

KATHERINE: Don't be silly.

ISOBEL: I want Irwin to go. But he won't.

IRWIN: Please, Isobel . . .

ISOBEL: I'm serious. He's threatening me.

> (ISOBEL *is watching* IRWIN *and the gun all the time now, not moving.* KATHERINE *makes a small move.*)

I want you just to walk out the door.

> (KATHERINE *frowns.*)

KATHERINE: Isobel, look, I don't get it.

ISOBEL: It doesn't matter. Find someone in the street.

KATHERINE: Are you sure? (*She smiles at* IRWIN *for approval.*)
Well, I mean . . .

ISOBEL: Tell them we have an intruder up here.

KATHERINE: He's hardly an intruder.

ISOBEL: Katherine, just do it. I'm telling you. Just get on with it now.

> (ISOBEL *has raised her voice. But* KATHERINE, *as she is about to accept this and move, sees* IRWIN *reach out and pick up the gun. She stops dead still.*)

KATHERINE: Lord.

> (*At once* ISOBEL *moves towards the bed.*)

ISOBEL: Then I'll go. Wait for me.

IRWIN: Isobel. No.

> (*She has picked up the big blue coat from the bed and now puts it on.* IRWIN *has called out to her in panic. Now she smiles down at her bare feet.*)

ISOBEL: I haven't got shoes. Still you can't have everything.

> (*She goes back to the main door. The gun is pointing at her back. She opens the door and just as she closes it behind her,* IRWIN *fires five times at the door. It is deafeningly loud. The door splinters. There is noise from the other side.*)

KATHERINE: No! No!

> (IRWIN *turns towards us, the gun now lowered. He looks beaten. There is a silence.* KATHERINE *moves towards the door and opens it.* ISOBEL *lies dead on the floor at the other side.*
> KATHERINE *looks a moment, then kneels down beside her.*
> IRWIN *slumps on to a chair.* KATHERINE *puts her hand gently on* ISOBEL'S *chest to feel for life.*)

IRWIN: It's over. Thank God.

(There is a silence. Then the light begins to grow strongly from behind. The sound of high summer. Birds singing. Strong shafts of sunlight hitting the tall windows of Robert's living room and, in front of them, all his furniture as we left it at the end of the previous act, covered in white shrouds, and spaced about with packing cases. KATHERINE's *flat moves away, and the next scene begins.)*

SCENE EIGHT

Robert's living room. MARION *is moving slowly round the room, removing the shrouds from each piece of furniture, uncovering them, one by one. She is in a black dress. The ritual of removing the covers takes time.* TOM *comes in, wearing a black suit. He is carrying a chair.*

MARION: Over there.

(He goes and puts it down. MARION *goes on taking off covers.)*

TOM: There.

MARION: Yes, that's right. Good. The carpet.

TOM: Yes. I'll unroll it. *(He moves towards the rolled-up carpet, pausing as he does to readjust the position of another chair.)* This here?

MARION: Yes, that's good.

(Another chair moved.)

TOM: And this?

MARION: Yes, that's perfect.

(Another.)

TOM: This?

*(*MARION *stands a moment, the sheets in her hand, surveying the room.)*

MARION: It's as I remember it.

*(*RHONDA *comes in, in a short black skirt and jumper.)*

RHONDA: There's a call from the Ministry.

MARION: I don't want to speak to them.

RHONDA: Fine.

*(*MARION *goes across and hands her the sheets.* RHONDA *goes out*

79

with them. TOM *is on his knees now, unrolling an old weathered carpet of many colours.*)

MARION: We played over there. Under the piano. Isobel had a kind of magic world.

(TOM *nods. Then* MARION *thinks, looking back towards the open door.*)

You must understand, Tom. I can't come to the church. (*He looks up, stopping in his work, also to think.* KATHERINE *comes in, dressed as she was for her husband's funeral. She is carrying a large vase of flowers.*)

KATHERINE: Flowers. Here we are.

TOM: That's wonderful.

MARION: Put them there.

(*She points to a table.* KATHERINE *sets them down.* MARION *is thoughtful.*)

Yes, they're fine.

KATHERINE: Thank you.

MARION: Good. (*She looks round a moment.*) When you were here, what else did you have?

KATHERINE: Oh, ornaments. I think. (*She gestures vaguely.*) Lamps and things. Well, everywhere.

(MARION *goes to a packing case and takes out vases and ornaments which she sets on side tables.*)

Robert loved things. It made me jealous. He'd pick up a book. Or a photograph. His whole mood would change. Right away. Things consoled him. He was lucky.

MARION: Yes.

KATHERINE: It's a gift.

(RHONDA *reappears at the door.*)

RHONDA: The people out there are waiting.

(MARION *is still surveying the room, adjusting objects, moving furniture.* TOM *has laid the carpet and is now standing.*)

RHONDA: They all want to walk in one group through the village. She does seem to have been amazingly popular.

(*There is pause.*)

It's like everyone valued her.

TOM: Yes.

MARION: Except us.

(*At once* TOM *makes a move towards her, alarmed.*)

TOM: Marion . . .

MARION: It's all right. We'll be with them in a moment. Katherine, come here.

(KATHERINE *walks across to her.* MARION *kisses her on the cheek.*)

We'll be out there in a moment. Just wait and we'll be along.

(RHONDA *and* KATHERINE *go in silence.* TOM *and* MARION *are left alone.*)

It's all obscure. It frightens me. What people want. Tom. It's frightened me, ever since I was a child. My memory of childhood is of watching and always pretending. I don't have the right equipment. I can't interpret what people feel.

(TOM *moves and stands behind her, wanting to console her.*)

I've stood at the side. Just watching. It's made me angry. I've been angry all my life. Because people's passions seem so out of control. (*She shakes her head slightly.*) You either say, 'Right, OK, I don't understand anything, I'll take some simple point of view, just in the hope of getting things done. Just achieve something, by pretending things are simpler than they are.' Or else you say, 'I will try to understand everything.' (*She smiles.*) Then I think you go mad.

TOM: It's not that bad. The Lord Jesus . . .

(*At once he stops.*)

MARION: Yes, Tom? The Lord Jesus what?

TOM: I don't know. I've slightly lost touch with the Lord Jesus.

(*He looks at her, then smiles. She smiles too. Then she gestures round the whole room. It is perfectly restored into an English sitting room – furniture, carpets, curtains, ornaments.*)

Yes. Well done. It's lovely.

(*There's a pause.*)

A perfect imitation of life.

(MARION *smiles and moves towards him. They embrace. He kisses her, with more and more passion. He undoes the buttons on the front of her dress and puts his hand inside, on her breasts. Then he runs his hand down the front of her body. She puts her head right back.*)

Oh God, you feel wonderful.

MARION: Yes, so do you.

(*They kiss again. Then he takes a couple of steps back, smiling, slightly adjusting his tie.*)

Tom. I love you.

TOM: I'll be back soon.

(*He pauses, and laughs a small laugh. Then turns and goes out. MARION is left alone. She sits on the sofa at the centre.*)

MARION: Isobel. We're just beginning. Isobel, where are you? (*She waits a moment.*) Isobel, why don't you come home?